The Unknown Life of Jesus Christ

Nicolas Notovitch

Translated by Virchand R. Gandhi
Translation revised by Professor G. L. Christie

DOVER PUBLICATIONS, INC.
Mineola, New York

Bibliographical Note

This Dover edition, first published in 2008, is an unabridged republication of the work published by Progressive Thinker Publishing House, Chicago, in 1907. The work was originally published in 1894 by V. R. Gandhi. Its original title was *The Unknown Life of Jesus Christ. From an ancient manuscript, recently discovered in a Buddhist monastery in Tibet by Nicolas Notovitch. Translated from the French and edited with an introduction and illustrations by Virchand R. Gandhi. Revised by Prof. G. L. Christie.*

Library of Congress Cataloging-in-Publication Data

Notovitch, Nicolas, b. 1858.
    [Vie inconnue. English]
    The unknown life of Jesus Christ / Nicolas Notovitch ; translated by Virchand R. Gandhi ; translation revised by G. L. Christie.
        p. cm.
    Originally published: Chicago : Progressive Pub. House, 1907.
    ISBN-13: 978-0-486-46853-2 (pbk.)
    ISBN-10: 0-486-46853-4 (pbk.)
    1. Jesus Christ—Biography—Apocryphal and legendary literature. 2. Christianity and other religions—Buddhism. I. Gandhi, Virchand Raghavji, 1864–   II. Christie, G. L. III. Title.

BT520.N6813 2008
232.9'01—dc22

                2008028446

Manufactured in the United States of America
Dover Publications, Inc., 31 East 2nd Street, Mineola, N.Y. 11501

Contents

The Vale of Kashmir. (*See page 4.*)

Illustrations

Shrinagar. (*See page 7.*)

Preface

Subsequent to the Turkish war (1877–1878) I undertook a series of journeys in the Orient. Having visited all the localities, more or less remarkable, of the Balkan Peninsula, I crossed the Caucasus mountain to Central Asia and Persia, and finally in 1887 I started for India, a most extraordinary country, which had attracted me from my early days.

The aim of my journey was to become acquainted with the inhabitants of India, and to study on the spot their manners and customs, the grand and mysterious archæology, and the colossal and majestic nature of this country. Wandering from one place to another, without a settled plan, I reached the mountainous Afghanistan, from where I reached India by the picturesque passes of Bolan and Guernai. Having ascended the Indus as far as Rawal Pindi, I crossed the Punjab, the country of the five rivers, and visited the Golden Temple of Armitsar and the tomb of Ranjit Sing, the king of the Punjab, near Lahore. I then directed my steps towards Kashmir, "the valley of eternal felicity." There in order to satisfy my curiosity, I recommenced my wanderings and continued them until I arrived at Ladak, whence I decided to return to Russia, through Karakorroum and Chinese Turkestan.

One day in the course of my visit to the Buddhist convent, situated on my route, I learnt from the chief Lama, that there existed in the archives of Lassa very ancient memoirs treating of the life of Jesus Christ and the nations of the Occident, and that certain great monasteries possessed copies and translations of those chronicles. As there was little probability that I should again visit those countries, I postponed to a future date my return to Europe, and, cost what it might, I resolved either to secure those copies from the great convents, or at any rate go to Lassa for further information on the subject—a journey far from being so dangerous and difficult as we are led to believe. Moreover, by this time I was so well accustomed to these kinds of perils that they could not deter me from my undertaking.

During my stay at Leh, the capital of Ladak, I visited the great monastery of Himis, situated near the city. The chief Lama of the monastery told me that the monastic library contained some copies of the manuscript in question. Lest I should awaken the suspicion of the authorities on the object of my visit to the convent, and thereby find obstacles in my character as a Russian in my future journey in Tibet, I determined to leave the capital of Ladak, and departed for India. An unfortunate fall, by which I broke my leg, furnished me with an unexpected pretext to return to the monastery, where I received excellent care; and during my short stay with the Lamas, I had the honor of obtaining the consent of their chief to have brought from the library the manuscript relating to Jesus Christ, and, aided by my interpreter, who translated for me from the Tibetan language, I wrote down carefully the verses as they were read by the Lama.

Not doubting at all the authenticity of this chronicle, related with great exactitude by the Brahmin historians and by the Buddhists of India and Nepal, I determined upon my return to Europe to publish the translation. With this object I addressed myself to several well-known ecclesiastics, requesting them to revise these notes, and to give me their opinion of them.

His Lordship, Bishop Platon, the celebrated Metropolitan of Kiew, admitted that this discovery was of great importance; he, however, endeavored to dissuade me from giving publicity to the memoirs, declaring that their publication would only injure me. Why? This the venerable prelate refused to tell me more explicitly. Our conversation, however, having taken place in Russia, where censure might have vetoed such a work, I determined to wait.

A year later I happened to be in Rome. There I submitted my

manuscript to a cardinal who has great influence with the Pope, and who answered me as follows: "What is the use of having that published; no one will attach any great importance to it, and you will only create numerous enemies. Nevertheless, you are still young. If it is a question of money which interests you, I can obtain for you a recompense in exchange for your notes which will remunerate you well for all expense and for the time lost." Naturally, I refused.

At Paris I spoke of my project to Cardinal Rotelli, whose acquaintance I had made at Constantinople. He also opposed the publication of my work under the pretext that it would be premature. "The church," he added, "suffers already too much from this new current of atheistic ideas, and you will only furnish new pasture to the culumniators and slanderers of the Evangelical doctrine. I say this in the interest of all Christian churches." After this I called on M. Jules Simon. He found that my communication was a very interesting one and recommended me to ask the advice of M. Rènan, upon the best way to publish the memoirs.

The next day found me in the office of the great philosopher. At the end of our conversation, M. Rènan proposed to me to intrust the memoirs in question to him, so that he might be able to make a report to the Academy. This position was, as anyone may easily understand, very tempting and flattering. I, however, carried away the work under the pretext of revising it once more. I foresaw in truth that if I accepted this combination, I would only enjoy the honor of having discovered the Chronicle, while the illustrious author of the "Life of Jesus" would have all the glory of the publication and the commentaries. Believing myself sufficiently well prepared to publish alone the translation of the Chronicles with notes, I declined the very gracious offer which M. Rènan had made. In order not to wound the susceptibility of the great master, for whom I entertained a profound respect, I resolved to wait till his death—a fatal event which could not be far distant, judging from his general feebleness.

A short time after the death of M. Rènan, I wrote to M. Jules Simon asking his advice. He replied that it was for me to avail myself of the opportunity that was presented for placing the memoirs before the public. I then put my notes in order, and am now having them published, reserving the right to affirm the authenticity of the chronicles. I set forth in my commentaries the argument which should convince us of the sincerity and good faith of the Buddhist compilers. I add that before criticising my work, the learned societies could, without much expense, organize a scientific expedition, having for its mission the study of these manuscripts on the spot and thus verify their historical value.

NICOLAS NOTOVITCH.

Translator's Introduction

The work, the translation of which I now put before the public, has created much comment among the thinking people all the world over, and journalists have written both favorable and hostile criticisms on it. I shall not devote the pages of this work to a consideration of those criticisms. Having, however, been born in India and traveled over that vast country, I feel it my duty to put before the reader some salient points which seem to me to have an important bearing on the facts set forth by the work.

I do not know why Christian theologians misrepresent the facts, which they can, if they intend to be truthful, put before the intelligent public in their true light. I can cite numerous instances in which reverend gentlemen have, intentionally or unintentionally, distorted, mangled and murdered the truth—I do not know with what object. The intelligent public of this country are well acquainted with the Rev. Dr. Edward Everett Hale, of Boston, and had I not known him at all I would have said that he had intentionally misrepresented the facts when he wrote an article in the North American Review (May, 1894) on "The Unknown Life of Jesus Christ;" but knowing, as I do, of his broad views and catholic spirit, I would simply attribute his statements in that article to ignorance on the subject. That Reverend gentleman, while criticizing this work (The Unknown Life of Jesus Christ), says: "But now Mr. Notovitch comes to the front and remembers that he has an excellent Life of Christ which he found in a somewhat mythical convent in Tibet, some years ago," meaning thereby the convent of Himis, where

Mr. Notovitch discovered the manuscripts, and further on: "he visited the convent of Himis, which we do not find on our own calendar of Buddhist ecclesiastical establishment near Leh, the capital of Ladak." Monstrous statements! The monastery of Himis is one of the most well-known institutions in Tibet, and very few persons who have traveled in Ladak have failed to visit that monastery. Professor Sir Monier Monier-Williams makes mention of this monastery in his work on Buddhism (p. 433, English edition, 1889) in these words: "Hence large monastic institutions are often found in solitary places and elevated situations; for instance, in Ladak those at Lama Yurru and *Himis* are more than 11,000 feet above the sea, and that at Hanle is 14,000 feet. They resemble romantic castles towering upwards in the midst of rocks, crags and snowy mountains." In the years 1854–58 a scientific mission was undertaken by the brothers Hermann, Adolphe and Robert de Schlagintweist to India and High Asia; they also visited various parts of Tibet and the Buddhist countries in the Himalaya. The first of them visited the monastery of Himis in September, 1856, and got an exact copy of a curious inscription relating to the founding of the institution, which is carved on a stone slab in the monastery, and of which I here give a copy and the translation for the information of my readers. I also give a picture of the monastery, so that they may be assured of its existence.

The inscription is divided into two paragraphs, the first of which begins with a hymn to the Buddhist triad:

"Hail! Praise be and benediction! Salutation to the teachers! To the most perfect, eminent Buddha, who has the characteristic signs and proportions; to the excellent law, which reveals the entire truth; to the congregation of the faithful, who endeavor to become delivered; all honor be to these three Supremacies after a prostration at the feet of the superiors [Lamas.]"

The remainder of the first paragraph relates the faithful adherence to Buddhism, of the founder of this monastery, Dharmaraja Senge Nampar Gyalva, and his father, and the universal reverence paid by the Ladakians to the holy triad. It is stated that Senge Nampar ordered to be built in his territory the "Vihara [monastery] of the three gems," on a magnificent style,

The Himis Monastery

ༀ་སྭསྟི། །དཀོན་མཆོག་གསུམ་ལ་ཕྱག་འཚལ་ལོ། །

The inscription in the Himis monastery

and named it "the Sangye chi ku sung thug chi ten," i.e. the support of the meaning of Buddha's precepts, "whence the sun of
the doctrine arose in this country brilliant as the dawn of the
day." It is further reported that in the reign of this monarch
many most learned and powerful Lamas had come to Ladak
and taught the doctrine. The names of some of them are
mentioned.

The second paragraph mentions that the erection of the convent was entrusted to Pal-dan-tsa-vai Lama, who had dwelt in
numerous monasteries, and had become firm and strong in the
ten commandments.

The edifice was commenced in the month Voda, in a certain
year which in the Tibetan astronomy is named "the male water-
horse year," and was finished in the "male water-tiger year,"
when the lama performed the ceremony of consecration, which
is a sign of completion. "In the male iron-dog year" were placed,
outside the enclosure, 300,000 prayer-cylinders. The document
concludes by alluding to the merits which the king, the work-
men (the masons, carpenters, porters) and, in fact, all engaged
in the construction of this monastery, had derived from their
assistance, and mentions in particular the salutary influence
which the monastery will exercise in future upon the welfare
and salvation of the inhabitants of Ladak. The monastery was
commenced in 1644 A.C. and finished in 1664.

If, nowithstanding these facts, the Himis monastery is "a
mythical convent" or that "we do not find [it] on our own calendar of Buddhist ecclesiastical institutions," the native of Central
Africa may as well say that Chicago is a city existing only in the
imagination of the Americans, or the inhabitant of the Fiji
islands may say he does not find Palestine on his own list of
Christian holy places. We can excuse these persons for their
ignorance, but not a Doctor of Divinity like Rev. Dr. Hale.

M. Notovitch, having in his journey broken his leg, was
obliged to stay for a short time at the monastery of Himis, where
he received medical aid. This hospitality of the Buddhist monks
is interpreted in a half sneering, half sarcastic way by Dr. Hale,
thus: "It was as if a Buddhist delegate to the Parliament of
Religions had been wounded in watching a Princeton foot-ball

match and Dr. McCosh had received him to his hospitality. What more natural than that Dr. McCosh should give his guest a New Testament?" To a person educated to think that he is insulted if a stranger happens to talk familiarly with him, without an introduction, Oriental hospitality may seem an improbability; but, despite the gratuitous assumptions of Western scholars who have never visited India, that hospitality is *still there*. It is in the hundreds of Dharmashalas [inns] erected by the Jains of India at most of their important towns, in which travelers can rest for a time free of charge, and at several places even meals can be had on the same terms. It is found, in the words of Sir William Hunter, "in that gentleness and charity to all men, which takes the place of a poor law in India, and gives a high significance to the half satirical epithet of the 'mild' Hindu."

I shall not dwell on other points misrepresented in Dr. Hale's article, dismissing them simply with the remark that it has been a sad fatality that Orientals and their religions, manners and customs have always been misconstrued by people who have no right to speak thereon without making a thorough study of them.

India has been the dreamland of many scholars. Students, philosophers and antiquarians see visions of India. More than a hundred years ago (August 1783) Sir William Jones saw a vision while standing alone on the deck of his vessel en route to India. "It gave me," he says, "inexpressible pleasure to find myself in the midst of so noble an amphitheatre, almost encircled by the vast regions of Asia, which has ever been esteemed the nurse of science, the inventress of delightful and useful arts, the scene of glorious actions, fertile in the productions of human genius, and infinitely diversified in forms of religion and government, in the laws, manners, customs, as well as in the features and complexions of men."

This grand man knew how to make his dream come true, and change his vision into a reality. He startled European scholars by his translation of Shakuntala, "One of the greatest curiosities," as he said in his preface, "that the literature of Asia has yet brought to light." He also translated the laws of Manu, founded the Asiatic Society of Bengal, and achieved marvelous results in the researches of ancient literature of India. Colebrook, H. H. Wilson, and many others followed him, and to-day we have a mass of Sanscrit and Prakrit literature, Hindu, Jain and Buddhist, lying before the European scholars, giving a clue to India's ancient history.

If we are proud of these learned scholars who have disclosed to the Western nations the ancient glory and civilization of India, we cannot help being ashamed of several short-sighted Europeans, and Americans too, who think that "India has no history worth mentioning until the time of the Mahomedan conquest"; "that Indian history is nothing but a dreary record of disunion and subjection," and who on the whole present to the public, India as a conquered country. But the careful student of Indian antiquities and literature is convinced that they present a history of Hindu civilization for thousands of years so full and clear "that he who runs may read."

The theory that Jesus at the age of thirteen went to India has been held by many to be true, but it is for the first time advanced publicly by M. Notovitch. Orthodox Christians would deem it sacrilegious even to imagine that the "Son of God" went to India and there studied its religions and philosophies. We shall examine the facts which will help us to reason on this point.

Christian divines have described India as a heathen country both materially and spiritually. Comparisons are frequently drawn between the civilization of Ancient India and Europe, and a missionary in India has taken great pains to show that Hindu civilization was nothing in comparison with modern Western civilization. He also thinks that the civilization of ancient India represented only the infancy of civilization. To him the glorious civilization of Europe is the model. In his opinion only the ignorant and half-educated look upon the past as the Golden, and the present as the Iron age; while he himself forgets his own doctrines on the original fall of man.

It is a giant mistake to compare the Hindu civilization with Western civilization. It is impossible to compare the industrial productions, hand wrought of India, with those of Europe, "turned out" as it is aptly phrased, by machines. Machinery and mechanical progress cannot be applied to any artistic work, except the avowed imitation or copying of great art works. It is true that the Hindu artist has his own traditions on decorative art, which is a crystalized tradition although perfect in form; it is true that the spirit of fine art which is latent in India, requires to be quickened into creative operations in these times. Still the Indian workman, from the humblest potter to the most cunning embroiderer in blue, purple, scarlet and gold, is a true artist. But has the Western civilization preserved his true character? Sir George Birdwood, who lived and studied in India for a number of years the native industries of that country, says in connection with the Indian exhibits in the Paris Exposition of 1878: "Indian collections are now also, unfortunately, becoming at every succeeding exposition, more and more over-crowded with mongrel articles, the result of the influences on Indian art, of English society, missionary schools, schools of art, and international exhibitions, and above all, of the irresistible energy of the mechanical productiveness of Manchester, Birmingham, Paris and Vienna."

Terry in his "Voyages to the East Indies," 1655, in describing the people of India writes: "The natives there show very much ingenuity in their curious manufactures, as in their silk stuffs, which they most artificially weave, some of them very neatly mingled with silver or gold, or both; as also in making quilts of their stained cloth or of fresh colored taffata lined with their printadoes (prints or chintz), or of their satin, lined with taffata, betwixt which they put pure cotton-wool, and work them together with silk. . . . They will make any new thing by pattern, howsoever difficult it may seem to be; it is therefore no marvel if the natives there make boots, clothes, linen, bands, cuffs of English fashion, which are all very different from their own fashions and habits, and yet make them all exceedingly neat."

I am not a supporter of the caste system as it exists to-day in India, but I am convinced, with Dr. Leitner, formerly the Registar of the Punjab University in India, that the preservation of caste in its original form is the preservation of ancient civilization and unparalleled culture of India, inclusive of its arts and industries, which is perfectly compatible with every legitimate demand of modern requirements or aspirations. "The recognition of the principle of heredity in abilities and defects, so tardily recognized by our own physiologists, has maintained Indian society, Indian wisdom, Indian bravery, and Indian arts, and can alone preserve Indian loyalty and ensure Indian progress on the lines of its own genius. It is only *imitation of foreign models* that can kill what thousands of years and the various vicissitudes of conquest have spared." Sir George Birdwood therefore says to the European public: "We therefore incur a great responsibility when we deliberately undertake to improve such a people in the practice of their own arts, and hitherto the results of our attempts to do so have been anything but encouraging. The Kashmir trade in shawls has been ruined through the quickness with which the weavers have adopted the 'improved shawl patterns' which the French agents of the Paris import houses have set before them, and presently we shall see what the effect of the teaching of our Schools of Art has been on Indian pottery, the noblest pottery in the world until we began to meddle with it. . . . We incur a great responsibility in attempting to interfere in the direct art education of a people who already possess the tradition of a system of decoration founded on perfect principles, which they have learned through centuries of practice to apply with unerring truth. . . . Of late these handicraftsmen, for the sake of whose works the whole world has been ceaselessly pouring its bullion for three thousand years into India, and who, for all the marvelous tissues and broidered work, have fouled no streams, nor poisoned any air; whose skill and individuality the training of countless generations has developed to the highest perfection; these hereditary handicraftsmen are being everywhere gathered from their democratic village community in hundreds and thousands to the colossal mills of Bombay to drudge in gangs at manufacturing piece-goods, in competition with Manchester, in the production of which they are no more intellectually or morally concerned than the grinder of a barrel organ in the 'tune it turns out.'"

The arts and sciences of India are not modern. Their origin is hidden in pre-historic times. Religion and philosophy have been the great contributions of India to the world, and they have drawn savants and philosophers to her in times, ancient and modern. Is it improbable then, that Jesus, too, might have visited India? But if he did, how, especially in times when there were no conveniences for traveling?

The ancient commerce of India with other countries had brought her people in close connection with those of others, who went to India either by sea or by the caravan route. Many people are skeptical as to there having been any intercourse, in those times, between India and the countries around the Mediterranean, but careful investigations of scholars have conclusively shown that India's gold and silver, precious stones, spices and silks had always attracted people of other countries to her. The Hindu and Jain Scriptures bear ample testimony to this—which to the average Christian reader are but myths, while the Bible is to him a veritable record of truth. We will proceed from his standpoint, and prove conclusively that the most valuable and complete notices of the ancient trade of India are in the Bible.

Moses about 1500 B.C., in Genesis II. 11–12, describing the first head, Pison, of the river of Eden says: "That is it which compasseth the whole land of Havilah, where there is gold. . . . There is b'dellium and the onyx stone." B'dellium is the gum resin of two varieties, both natives of Sindh in India; cinnamon mentioned in Proverbs VII. 17, and Song of Solomon IV. 14, is the product of Ceylon. In Numbers XXIV. 6, Balaam compares the camp of Israel to "A garden by the riverside as the trees of lign-aloes which the Lord hath planted, and as cedar trees beside the waters." This lign-aloes is the most precious of all perfumes known in Sanskrit, Agaru, and in the Hebrew Ahalim and Ahaloth. In the Song of Solomon (Circa B.C. 1000) IV. 13–14, mention is made, besides of myrrh, aloes, cinnamon, frankincense and calamus, of camphire saffron and spikenard, in this and also in I. 14, camphire, the Hebrew copher, is the Egyptian hennah, a native of East India. The saffron, in the Hebrew karkan, the Sanskrit *kunkuma,* is a native of Kashmir, and spikenard is exclusively a native of Nepal and Bhotan at great elevations. The costus of Psalms XIV. 8, translated by Cassia in the English Bible, is also exclusively a native of Kashmir. These three famous products of the Himalayas, with b'dellium, the vine, pomegranate, lign-aloes, salep, hemp and musk, and the Balas ruby, lapis-lazuli and turquoise have been known from the earliest associations with the Aryans of India, whence saffron and hemp have followed their migrations everywhere throughout the temperate zone of the globe. The sandalwood used by Solomon for flooring and pillars is a native of India and the Eastern Archipelago only. The word "cotton" is not used in the English translation of the Bible; but in the passage of Esther (Circa B.C. 450) I. 6, "There were white, *green* and blue hangings," the Hebrew word translated *green* is *Karpos,* identical with Sanskrit *Karpasa* and Hindi *Kapas,* cotton, an aboriginal Indian production. The passage should be read: "There were white and blue (striped) cotton hangings," like the *sattrangis* made all over Hindustan at the present day.

Opium, hemp, tin and many other things were known by Homer in their Sanskrit names. The peacocks mentioned I. Kings X. 22, and II. Chronicles IX. 21, along with ivory and apes are true Indian peacocks as is proven by the Hebrew word used for them, *tukkiyim* being identical with the Sanskrit word *tokki* for peacocks. The Hebrew word *koph* here used for apes is also the Sanskrit *kapi.* Iron is frequently mentioned in the Bible under the Hebrew name of *paldah,* which is the Arabic *fulad* and indicates Indian iron. Homer mentions tin by its Sanskrit name *kasttra,* and the Phœnicians, who first learned the name from the trade through the Arabs with India, afterwards gave the name of Cassiterides to the Scilly Islands and Cornwall, where it still survives in Cassiter street, Bodmin. Homer's triple-gemmed ear-rings, Illiad XIV. 183, and Odessy, XVIII. 298, are the emerald ear-rings of India.

The pomegranate, the vine and the Soma are indirectly connected with the development of the Indian trade. The pomegranate is a native of Northwestern India, whence it was carried by the earliest Aryan emigrations into Media and Syria, and afterwards by the Phœnicians and the Carthaginians, from whence its Latin name Punica Granatum is derived. It is constantly represented on the sculptures of Assyria and Egypt with grapes and peaches, and is frequently mentioned in the Bible (Ex. XXVIII. 33–34; XXXIX. 24–26; Numb. XIII. 23; XX. 5; Deut.

VIII. 8; I Kings VII. 18; Song of Sol. IV. 3, 13.) The *Soma*, the renowned drink of the Vedas, and *hom* of the Zend Avesta, is indigenous to the Punjab and the Bolan pass, Khandesh, and the Ghats of Western India and Caromandel Coast; and from the sacred rites and rejoicings which accompanied the drinking of its fermented sap in Vedic times, and which are still celebrated among the Brahmins of India, it evidently was the first intoxicant discovered by the Brahmins. The division of the Persians from the Brahmins was the result of a dispute over the use of Soma as a religious service, particularly in the ceremony which symbolized the intoxication of the gods, which the Persians resolutely resisted. In the Caucasus mountains and Armenia the use of soma gradually passed into the use of wine (Gen. IX. 21), a fact which suggests an explanation of the true Brahmin origin of Bacchus and of the Dionysiac rites of ancient Greece. In the valley of the Tigris and Euphrates, the sap of the date palm particularly was substituted for that of *Soma* or *hom* as an intoxicating drink. There is a verse in the Rig Veda IX. celebrating the virtues of Soma, a finer Bacchic burst cannot be met with among the most enthusiastic of poets who have sung of wine: "O, Soma! there is nothing so bright as thou. When poured out, thou welcomest all gods, to bestow on them immortality. . . . The praiseworthy Soma has from ancient times been the drink of the gods; he was milked from the hidden recesses of the sky; he was created for Indra and was extolled. . . . In that realm where there is perennial light, and where the heaven is placed, O Soma, send me to that deathless and immortal realm! Flow thou for Indra."[1]

These facts prove the pre-historic antiquity of the trade of India with the West; it originated through Persia, Media, Mesopotamia, Syria and Asia Minor with the exodus of the Aryan race from Central Asia, as the philologists infer, from the names of various spices, drugs, vegetables, stones, etc. We also know that the ship captains of Solomon and Hiram not only brought Indian apes, peacocks, and sandal-wood to Palestine, they also brought their Sanskrit names. This was about 1000 B.C.

---

[1] Sir George Birdwood's Handbook.

The Assyrian monuments show that the rhinoceros and elephant were among the tribute offered to Shalmaneser II. (859–823 B.C.) The Greek historian Hekataios, of Miletos, (549–486 B.C.) speaks clearly of India. Herodotos, too, (450 B.C.) had some knowledge of India; and since Alexander's invasion (327 B.C.) the knowledge of the Western nations about India has become a matter of history. After Alexander's death his empire was partitioned, and Bactria and India fell eventually to Seleukos Nikator, the founder of the Assyrian monarchy, (323 B.C.). While Seleukos reigned in Syria from 312 to 280 B.C., Chandra Gupta reigned in the Gangetic valley from 316 to 292 B.C. In 312 B.C., Seleukos having recovered Babylon, proceeded to re-establish his authority in Bactria and the Punjab. After a war with Chandra Gupta, Seleukos ceded the Greek settlements to the Indian king and left Megasthenes as an ambassador at the Gangetic court. He also gave his daughter to Chandra Gupta in marriage.

We see, therefore, that, long before Jesus was born, India had become a familiar topic with the Western people. Alexander had brought Greece and India face to face; his officers wrote descriptions of different parts of his route, which have since perished, but they furnished materials to Strabo, Pliny and Arrian. Arrian gives a minute account of the sea-borne trade of India. Megasthenes, on the other hand, has left a life-like picture of the Indian people.

THE CARAVAN ROUTES.—The manuscript discovered by M. Notovitch gives us a clear account of Jesus from 12 to 26. It says that he went to India with a caravan of merchants. Are there any grounds to suppose that he did so?

We know as a fact that the earliest trade between the East and the West was carried on by caravans, and long after the sea-routes by the Red Sea and the Persian Gulf began to be used, the land trade continued to be more important than the sea-borne. The earliest of these caravan routes were those between Egypt, Arabia and Assyria, and these are referred to in the Bible. In Gen. II. 11–12, we are told of the land of Havilah, that there was gold there, and b'dellium and the onyx stone. Havilah is in Arabia Felix, to the north of Ophir, and the passage simply indicates the route through which the b'dellium or musk of India was received in Egypt in the time of Moses. The passage, Psalms XIV. 8: "All thy garments smell of myrrh, aloes and cassia, out of the ivory palaces, whereby they have made thee glad," is generally supposed to allude to the tablets and alabasters or scent-bottles in which perfumes were kept in ancient times. But it may also be translated "Out of the ivory palaces of the Minæans," a people of Arabia Felix, who, like their neighbors, the Sabæans and the Gerrhæans on the Persian Gulf, were the chief carriers of the Indian trade, and renowned in all ancient times for their fabulous opulence and luxury. In Gen. XXXVII. 25, we read that the sons of Israel sat down in Dothan to eat bread, "and they lifted up their eyes and looked, and behold a company of Ishmaelites came from Gilead with their camels, bearing spicery and balm and myrrh, going to carry it down to Egypt," and that as the "Midianites, merchantmen" passed by, "his brethren sold Joseph to the Ishmaelites," who were probably traveling by the immemorial caravan route, through Canaan and Edom and Midian, from Chaldœa into Egypt, the route by which Israel afterwards sent his sons into Egypt with balm and honey, spices and myrrh, nuts and almonds, for a present to "the man," their brother, who was now governor over the land. Many beautiful and sublime scripture images are taken from this trade, as in Isaiah LXIII. 1, "Who is this that cometh out of the wilderness like pillars of smoke, perfumed with myrrh and frankincense, with all powders of the merchant? . . . They hold all swords, being expert in war, every man hath his sword upon his thigh, because of fear in the night;" passages giving also a vivid picture of a Mecca caravan of the present day, and of the dangers besetting it, with its rich merchandise of China, India and Persia.

As we learn from the account of the wars, both of Moses and of Gideon with the Midianites, they were a very wealthy Arab people, living partly by predatory incursions into the neighboring territories, and partly by carrying on a caravan trade, across the intervening deserts, with the powerful states of Egypt and Chaldæa.

There was an immemorial commerce between India and the

nations of the Mediterranean and there were several routes followed at different times. The route by Kirman Gerrha and Petra was probably the oldest of all. In those early times the produce of India came to Kirman and Ormuz and was thence carried across the Persian Gulf to Gerrha, the emporium of the pearl fishery still carried on among Bahrein Islands, the ancient Tylos and Aradus, which with Muscat, were the original sets of those seafaring Arabs, who afterwards established themselves in Phœnicia and carried their settlements from port to port along the eastern and southern shores of the Mediterranean from Tyre to Sidon to the coast of Mauritania.

In India, Pattala—the modern Thattha on the river Indus in Sindh, was in early times a place of great importance—the point where all the caravan routes in India, and leading into India, converged. It was near to this spot that Alexander crossed the Indus, and here also the different lines from China, through the Kashmir valley, and from Sarmatia (now Russia), Media and Mesopotamia, through the Bamian and Khaiber passes first entered India. Sindh was therefore the place where a caravan of foreign merchants would first halt in India.[2] This confirms the statement in the Buddhist manuscript of the life of Jesus that He first went to Sindh.

Besides the caravan route, there were two other routes—the Persian Gulf route and the Red Sea route. The Bible is full of references to the trade by these routes also. Jerusalem was in early times an important place of commerce and the rivalry between Jerusalem and Edom finds a striking expression in the Bible throughout the whole period of prophetic development among the Hebrews, as in Isaiah XXXIV. 5–6; Jeremiah XLIX. 13–22; Ezekiel XXV. 13–14, and XXXV. 15; and Amos I. 10–12.

The crowning proof of the Indian trade with the countries on the shores of the Mediterranean and the Red Seas before the birth of Jesus, is offered from the fact that during the reign of Ptolemy Euergetes (B.C. 145–116), a Hindu was found on the Egyptian coast of the Red Sea in a boat by himself, speaking a language unknown to the people of that country, and whose ship

---

[2] I am indebted for much of this information to Sir George Birdwood.

had been wrecked there. The prominent headland on the southeast coast of Arabia is named *Ras-el-Kabir-Hindi*—"The Cape of the Hindu's Grave"—from the fact that navigation was considered dangerous in those times by the Arabs. The castaway Hindu, however, on being taken to Alexandria, offered to pilot an Egyptian ship back to India by the voyage he had himself made, and Euxodus was sent on this voyage of discovery, and reached India and returned safely to Egypt with a cargo of spices and precious stones. The greatest skeptic must admit that the land and sea-borne trade of India had given her a worldwide fame not only for her gold, spices and silk, but for her religions and philosophies also.

Buddha, the founder of Buddhism, died in 543 B.C., and Mahavira, the last Arhat of the Jains, in 526, that is, 17 years later. Jainism has been known to have existed even before the time of Buddha and therefore is the oldest missionary religion in the history of the world. Ashoka the Great, the Emperor of Northern India, was converted to the faith of Buddha in 257 B.C., and his grandson, Samprati, later on was converted to Jainism. The grandfather and the grandson have done for their respective religions what Constantine has done for Christianity. Ashoka has left a number of edicts in the form of inscriptions cut on rocks, caves and pillars and in the language and alphabet of the time, and scattered all over India. The famous French scholar Separt has recently published these inscriptions in his learned work "Les Inscriptions de Piyadasi." From the thirteenth inscription, which mentions the names of Antiochus of Syria, Ptolemy of Egypt, Antigonus of Macedon, Magas of Cyrene, and Alexander of Epiros, it appears that these kings were contemporaries of Ashoka and that they made treaties with him, and with their permission he sent Buddhist missionaries to preach his religion in those countries. Ashoka's grandson sent missionaries to many foreign countries to preach Jainism and often the monks of one religion were mistaken for those of the other, by reason of a close similarity in dress and ceremonial observances. These religions were therefore well-known in Egypt, Syria, Greece and other places, long before Jesus was born. "Buddhist missionaries," says a Christian writer, "preached in Syria two centuries before the teaching of Christ (which has so many moral points in common) was heard in northern Palestine. So true is it that every great historical change has had its forerunner."

It is beyond doubt, therefore, that India was commercially connected with the countries situated on the shores of the Mediterranean many centuries before the birth of Jesus; that India's wealth and commodities had attracted different people to her in very ancient times; that her religions were openly preached and known in the very land which afterwards became the birth-place of Jesus; that Alexander's conquest had made foreign nations more familiar with India and her people and her glory had spread throughout *the world then known.* Is it then impossible that Jesus, having heard of the richness of the philosophies and sciences of India, should have gone there with a desire to study them? Add to this the various passages, both in the Old and New Testaments, which bear a close resemblance with the Buddhistic, Hindu and Jain thoughts, (nay, some of the very customs and practices of the Jews of those early times can be fully explained only in the light of Indian wisdom) and the evidence is overwhelming in favor of the theory that Jesus must have been attracted to and lived in India during the time about which the Evangelists are silent.

In connection with the original work, in French, of M. Notovitch, I have very little to say. In the first part of his book, "Journey to Tibet," he gives a very minute description of the hills, gorges, rivers, etc., over which he traveled, which is tedious to the average reader. I have, therefore, abridged that part, and have described his journey in my own words, omitting nothing that is at all interesting; on the contrary, I have added many things which M. Notovitch could not, he being a foreigner in the East, and therefore not well acquainted with its people and their customs. I have illustrated the work with many pictures—which I hope will make the book acceptable to all readers.

The summary which appears at the end of the book, I have given verbatim, but have added several footnotes.

M. Notovitch, being a foreigner in India, is not expected to be an authority on the religions, manners or customs of her people.

Like other foreigners he has formed incorrect notions, especially on such subjects for which he had to refer to works written by Europeans. I have, therefore, pointed out these facts in the footnotes.

VIRCHAND R. GANDHI
Chicago, June 1894

Journey to Tibet

During the sojourn of M. Notovitch in India, he enjoyed frequent opportunities of mingling and holding converse with Buddhists, and the many interesting accounts which they gave him of Tibet so enthused him that he decided to take a journey to that still unexplored country.

With this object he chose a route leading through the enchanting valley of Kashmir—a country which he had often desired to visit.

Leaving Lahore October 14th, 1887, he arrived at Rawal Pindi the following day, where he made all preparations for a long and tedious journey over a region where railroads are unknown, and where the only means of conveyance are horses—a journey more or less fraught with dangers from incomplete roads through rugged mountains, and the possible prey of wild animals with which the forests abound.

Often the traveler may journey many weary miles without finding an inn where he may rest, except the isolated bungalows, which have been erected at intervals along the road by the English; these are small houses with one floor, not particularly attractive for their comforts, but to the traveler, exhausted from climbing over the rugged and dangerous mountain-roads, these bungalows where he may find shelter and rest appear even as a luxury.

It is not my intention to relate in detail all the incidents of this journey of M. Notovitch, which are sometimes tedious; nor shall I dwell on the glowing descriptions of the grand and magnificent mountain gorges, and the picturesque landscapes made glorious by the songs of myriads of gay-plumaged birds which one beholds with admiring eyes at every step in the forests; nor shall I attempt a description of the gorgeous sunsets which, renowned travelers concede, cannot be seen so glorious elsewhere in all the world as in the Himalayas; not even Italy with all her immortal fame with which great artists have justly adorned her, can boast of such inexpressible grandeur as is displayed at sunset in these mountains. The perfectly pure atmosphere, the deep blue sky, against which the towering snow-capped peaks resemble huge masses of glittering silver, gold and diamonds, fantastically wrought, are scenes which intoxicate the senses of man with their ravishing beauty, and he is utterly incapable of describing with tongue or pen the magnificence of their splendors or the holy emotions with which the soul is inspired.

I will confine myself to a faithful account of M. Notovitch's journey, giving all the points of interest touched upon by him.

Leaving the valley of the Punjab, M. Notovitch, with his retinue, climbed the steep winding road, penetrating the counterforts of the Himalayas, descending at sunset to the little town of Marri, which stands at an altitude of 7,457 feet, and is quite a summer resort for English officials and their families. Thence they descended after nightfall, resting a few hours at a bungalow, continuing the journey at dawn, reaching the hamlet Tong at noon, at which place M. Notovitch hired a Hindu cabriolet, which conveyance he failed to enjoy on account of the cramped position in which he was obliged to sit "like a Turk." He managed, however, to reach Hori in this kind of carriage, at which place he changed his mode of travel and secured saddle-horses.

I will here relate an experience which M. Notovitch had at the little hamlet where he halted to rest and lunch, and where provisions and all sorts of merchandise were sold. He approached a Hindu, who was squatted before a kettle of boiling milk and after having examined it somewhat cautiously to be sure that it was milk, he wanted to purchase a glassful of it, whereupon the merchant offered him the kettle and its contents; at this our traveler remonstrated, saying that he only desired one glass of it;

M. Notovitch on the march

it was there that he learned his first lesson in orthodox Brahminism. "According to our laws," said the Hindu, "if a stranger or one not belonging to our caste, touches, gazes or points his finger at our food, by such act it is polluted and we cannot eat it. We must, not only throw it away, but must thoroughly cleanse and purify the utensil." This will, of course, seem perfectly absurd to the people of the West, but there are, I may add, deep metaphysical laws underlying many of these seemingly useless ceremonies, which would not be understood by the reader without a thorough study. I will not, therefore, attempt to explain them here.

M. Notovitch resumed his journey and reached next evening the celebrated valley of Kashmir. This "happy valley" is situated between the ranges of the Himalaya mountains and is about eighty-five miles long and twenty-five wide, through the length of which wind in a serpentine course the sparkling waters of the river Jhelum.

This valley is, no doubt, the most beautiful in the world, with its placid lakes, its sparkling rivers (on which are hundreds of floating houses, in which live as many families the year round), its fairy-like gardens floating on the lakes, its hills and islands covered with antique buildings, and its happy, easy-going, picturesque inhabitants, both male and female, robed in long white gowns with full loose flowing sleeves—the men with snow-white turbans, the women with little caps or bonnets, all of whom spend their time in their numerous devotional exercises or quietly working on their celebrated shawls or working curious designs in gold and silver, for which there is but a dull market these days of rapid machine imitations; and above all, the balmy atmosphere of this 'garden of the gods' conspires to make one forget all his troubles, real or imaginary.

There are legends extant regarding this valley, one of which claims that in very ancient times this valley was a great lake, and that an invading king ordered his men to make a passage between two rocks in a gorge, thereby draining the lake of its waters and ruining the adjacent country, by which he gained victory over the inhabitants. Another legend is, that the waters themselves forced a passage between the rocks of a gorge, leaving nothing of the great lake except a few lagoons and the river Jhelum.

M. Notovitch reached Shrinagar, the capital of Kashmir, on the evening of October 19th, where he remained six days, spending the time in making long excursions into the surrounding country, examining old ruins and studying the peculiar customs of the people.

The history of Kashmir is full of interesting incidents. I will give only a short sketch.

A Mahomedan writer, Noor-ul-deen, who begins the history of Kashmir with the Creation, affirms that the valley was visited by Adam after the fall; that the descendants of Seth reigned over the country for 1,110 years; and that after the deluge it became peopled by a tribe from Turkistan. The Hindu historians add that after the line of Seth became extinct, the Hindus conquered the country and ruled it until the period of the deluge, and that the Kashmirians were afterwards taught the worship of one God by Moses.[1]

It appears from chronicles actually existing that Kashmir has been a regular kingdom for a period far beyond the limits of history in general. From the year 2666 B.C. to 1024 A.C. it had been governed by princes of Hindu and Tartar dynasties, and their names have been duly handed down to posterity. In the reign of Ashoka, about the third century before Christ, Buddhism was introduced, and after remaining there for some time, under Tartar princes, the religion of the country was again succeeded by Hinduism. In the middle of the fourteenth century the Mahomedans appeared on the scene and annexed for a time Tibet to the kingdom of Kashmir. Sikander, one of the Mahomedan monarchs, destroyed the Hindu temples and images by fire and forced the people, at the point of the bayonet, to adopt the Mahomedan faith. At the end of the sixteenth century Akbar conquered this province. He took a fatherly interest in the people, but the loyalty of his children was but short-lived, as certain persons raised an insurrection. In 1752, the country passed from the possession of the Mogul throne and

---

[1] "The Diary of a Pedestrian."

fell under the rule of the Duranis, and for many years was convulsed by a series of wars and rebellions and subject to numerous governors. In 1813, Ranjit Sing, the Lion of the Punjab, became one of the recognized princes of India, and subdued the province of Kashmir. The Sikhs ruled for a time and after the English invasion of the Punjab, it came under the British rule. The English, however, in consideration of $3,750,000, handed over the unfortunate Kashmirians to the tender mercies of Gulab Sing, an attendant and counsellor of Ranjit Sing, "the most thorough ruffian that ever was created—a villain from a kingdom down to a half-penny," and the "Paradise of the Indies" was relinquished by England and forever, as was then supposed. But only a few years ago the present Maharaja was deprived of his powers by the British Government, and the country is now under British protection.

The "happy valley" of Kashmir does not possess the glory and prosperity that it did under the Mogul emperors, whose court enjoyed here the sweetness of pleasure in the midst of the pavilions, still standing on the islands of the lake. This was a great resort for the princes of Hindustan, who formerly came to spend the summer months, and to enjoy the magnificent and unrivaled festivals given by the Moguls. But time has wrought sad changes for this valley and its former glory. I will add, however, that notwithstanding these changes, the Kashmirians have wonderfully preserved their artistic skill and mechanical talent. Kashmir shawls have attained a world-wide reputation. At the Paris Exposition of 1878 was exhibited, with other wonderful Indian products, a shawl worked with a map of the city of Shrinagar, showing its streets and houses, its gardens and temples, with people interspersed here and there, and boats on the calm blue waters of the river, giving a clear life-like picture as in a photograph. Another shawl was one mass of the most delicate embroidery, representing the conventional Persian and Kashmir wilderness of flowers, with birds of the loveliest plumage singing among the bloom, and wonderful animals, and wondering men.[2]

---

[2] Reports of the Paris Exposition.

In fact, the embroidery on wool of Kashmir, both loom and hand-wrought, is of historical and universal fame. Elaborately chased goblets, rosewater sprinklers, in ruddy gold and parcel-gilt, testify to the Kashmir goldsmith's skill. The finest gemmed and enamelled jewelry in India is that of Kashmir. The enumeration in Isaiah III. 17–24 of the articles of the *mundus muliebris* of the daughters of Zion reads like an inventory of the exceedingly classical looking jewelry of Kashmir. The lacquered *papier mache* of Kashmir is the choicest in India.

Constant invasions and plunders have reduced the Kashmirians to poverty. They still retain much of their proud mien—the men are strongly built, the women the most beautiful in the world with their clear white complexions and haughty bearing.

Shrinagar, the capital, sometimes called Kashmir, is situated on the banks of the Jhelum, along which it extends the distance of about three miles; the houses of two stories in which live a population of 100,000 inhabitants, border the banks of the river, which is spanned by several bridges; the city is a little over a mile in width; steps lead from the houses to the waters of the Jhelum, where all the day people are to be seen performing their sacred ablutions, bathing or cleansing their utensils of copper. One part of the inhabitants are followers of the Mahomedan religion, two-thirds are Hindus, with a few Buddhists interspersed among them.

Manufacturers of shawls, gun-makers, workers in leather and papier mache, jewelers, tailors, shoe-makers, watch-menders, in fact all sorts of artisans, remarkable for their mechanical talent are to be found in this city. A visit to the show-rooms of shawl-merchants is a pleasure to the traveler.

Around the city there are several interesting places. The Tukht-i-Suliman or Solomon's Throne is an old Hindu temple, the oldest in Kashmir, situated upon a hill, 1,000 feet above the plain. Its erection is ascribed to Jaloka, the son of Ashoka, who reigned in the third century before Christ. The fort of Hari Parvat is another interesting sight; built by Akbar in 1597 A. C., at a cost of $5,000,000.

On the morning of October 27th, M. Notovitch left this interesting city to journey towards Tibet, adding to his retinue by

Solomon's Throne (*See page 7.*)

purchasing a large dog which had previously made the journey in company with the well-known explorers, Bon Valot, Capus and Pepin.

Upon reaching the chain of mountains which separate the valley of Kashmir from the gorge of Sind, the party were obliged to crawl on all fours almost all the way over a summit of 3,000 feet high; the carriers were quite exhausted from their heavy loads and from the fear of rolling down the deep declivity.

Descending from this point they passed through several villages, Chokodar, Dras, Karghil, etc., halting only at these places for rest or to procure fresh horses. Karghil is the chief town of the district and the scenery is certainly picturesque. It is situated on the confluence of the Suru and Wakha rivers, the view of which on its left side is one of the most striking the traveler can ever behold.

M. Notovitch procured fresh horses here and continued his journey over a route far from being pleasant or safe, sometimes passing over a very dangerous road, at other times being obliged to cross a shaky bridge consisting, as many bridges do in Kashmir, of two long beams or trunks of trees inserted in the crevices of the rocks on either bank and small poles or stones laid across, sometimes fagots being thrown on the poles and the whole covered with earth. The traveler, when crossing this point, might well tremble at the thought of a possible dislodgement of a stone or the oscillation of the beams which would precipitate the whole construction into the yawning chasm beneath.

M. Notovitch entered the boundaries of Ladak or Little Tibet and was much astonished to find a sweet, simple, happy people who did not indulge in or know what quarreling was. Especially was he astonished at this since polyandry flourishes there among the low-class people. Polyandry is a subject on which different writers have risked their opinions without knowing the facts. It is true that among the non-Aryan hill-tribes this custom has existed for centuries and the Hindu rulers did not interfere with them. They relied not on forcing their views upon a people but on educating them to it. The hill tribes who follow the custom of polyandry are isolated communities and socially have no connection with the Hindus. The trans-Himalayan tribes, too, follow this custom which has existed among them for a long time.

In Ladak, among the low-class people, each woman has from three to five husbands and that in the most legitimate manner in the world. It is the custom, when a man marries a woman she becomes the legal wife of all his brothers. If there is but one son in the family he usually marries into a family where there are already two or three husbands, and never but one wife. The days of each husband are fixed in advance and each acquits himself of his duties promptly in the most agreeable manner. The men are not long-lived or so robust as the women.

This practice existed long before Buddhism was introduced into that country, which religion is gradually uprooting the practice which is scarcely sanctioned among the more intelligent or better classes. From the description given by M. Notovitch it is evident that like other foreign travelers he has formed his opinions of the people from those with whom he came in contact. I know full well how difficult it is for a foreigner to get access to the better classes of Oriental society; in very rare instances, where one has influence with a native of high standing, has he the opportunity to see or know the better side.

We will leave polyandry and follow our traveler in his journey. From Karghil he went to the village of Surghol, twenty miles from the former and standing on the banks of the Wakha. Near it are to be seen masses of rocks forming long broad walls, upon which have been thrown, in apparent disorder, flat stones of various colors and sizes, on which are engraved all sorts of prayers in Urdu, Sanskrit and Tibetan characters.

Leaving Surghol with fresh horses, M. Notovitch made the next halt at the village of Wakha. Upon an isolated rock overlooking the village, stands the convent of Moulbek. With his interpreter and the negro servant he proceeded to this convent; they climbed the narrow steps, carved in the solid rock, on which were placed little prayer-wheels, which are little drumlike shapes covered round the sides with leather and fitted vertically in niches cut in the rock. A spindle running through the center enables them to revolve at the slightest touch or breeze; there are usually several of these wheels in a row, larger ones are placed separate, all are decorated on the leather bands with the mystic sentence—"Om mani padme hum," i.e. Om, the jewel in the lotus, amen!

On the top he was greeted by a Lama, attired in the usual monk's robe of yellow, with a cap of the same material, carrying in his right hand a prayer-wheel made of copper, which he twirled from time to time with his left hand, without interrupting the conversation. The Lama conducted the visitor through long, low rooms and halls into an open terrace, where as soon as they were seated attendants brought refreshments.

The Tibetan language is spoken here. It is only in the monasteries that the Tibetan is spoken in its purity.

The Lamas prefer visits from Europeans to those from Mahomedans. The reason of this preference is, as the Lama said:

"The Mahomedans have no point of contact with our religion; in their recent victorious campaign they converted by force many Buddhists to Islamism; it will require great efforts to bring back these descendants of Buddhists into the way of the true God. As for the Europeans, it is an entirely different matter. Not only do they profess the essential principles of monotheism, but they also are a part of the worshipers of Buddha under almost the same title as the Tibetan Lamas. The only error of the Christians is that after having adopted the great doctrine of Buddha, they completely separated themselves from him and created a different Dalai Lama. Ours alone has received the divine favor of seeing face to face the majesty of Buddha and the power to serve as meditator between the earth and the heaven."

"Who is this Dalai Lama of the Christians, of whom you have just spoken?" asked M. Notovitch to the Lama. "We have a Son of God to whom we address our fervent prayers, and it is to him that we have recourse so that he may intercede for us to our only and indivisible God."

"He is not the one in question here, Sahib. We also respect him whom you recognize as the Son of an only God, but we do not regard him as such but as the excellent being chosen from among all; Buddha, in truth, incarnated himself with his intelligence in the sacred person of Issa, who without the aid of either fire or sword went forth to spread our grand and true religion throughout the world. I allude to your earthly Dalai Lama—to whom you give the title of the Father of the Church. There lies the great sin: Is he able to save the sinners who are on the wrong road?" began the Lama twirling his prayer-wheel. Of course, he alluded to the Pope.

"You have just told me that a son of Buddha, Issa, had been chosen to spread your religion over the world. Who then is he?" asked M. Notovitch.

The Lama was amazed at the question but said in reply: "Issa is a great prophet, one of the first after the twenty-two Buddhas; he is greater than all the Dalai Lamas, for he constitutes a part of the spirituality of God. It is he who has instructed you, who brings back the frivolous souls to the knowledge of God, who has rendered you worthy of the blessings of the Creator, and who has endowed each being with the knowledge of good and evil; his name and deeds have been recorded in our sacred writings, and, while reading of his great life spent in the midst of erring people, we weep over the horrible sin of those heathens who assassinated him after putting him to the most cruel tortures."

M. Notovitch was struck by the words of the Lama—the prophet Issa, his tortures, his death, the Christian Dalai Lama and the recognition of Christianity by the Buddhists—all this made him think more and more of Jesus Christ; and he begged his interpreter to omit none of the words of the Lama. He asked the Lama where those sacred writings could be found and who had written them.

"The principal rolls," said the Lama, "which have been compiled in India and Nepal at different times according to the course of events, are to be found at Lassa and number several thousands. In some of the larger convents there are copies made by the Lamas at different times during their sojourn at Lassa and presented to their convents in remembrance of their sojourn with the great master, our Dalai Lama."

"Do you not possess any of these copies relating to the prophet Issa?"

"No, we have none of them. Our convent is rather unimportant and since its foundation our successive Lamas have only collected a few hundred works for their own use. The great cloisters possess thousands of them but they are sacred things and they will not show them to you."

They conversed together a little longer, after which M. Notovitch retired to the camp, reflecting deeply on all the words of the Lama. Issa, the prophet of the Buddhists! But how could that be? Being of the Jewish origin he lived in Palestine and Egypt, and the Scriptures contain not a word, not the slightest allusion to the role which Buddhism must have played in the education of Jesus.

He decided to visit all the convents of Tibet, hoping to gather more ample information concerning the prophet Issa, and perhaps find copies of the documents in question.

Our traveler continued his journey, crossing the pass of Namikula, 13,000 feet high. He arrived at the village of Lamieroo where he put up at an inn just under the windows of a convent, where he was immediately visited by several monks who plied him with many questions as to the route he came by, the object of his journey, etc., etc.

Lamieroo, as the name would imply, was the headquarters for the Lamas and their religion for many years. Upon the extreme top ledge of a precipice of concrete stone stands the old monastery, curious enough in its construction of stone, overlooking the village some hundred feet below, the houses being perched on pinnacles of rock and scattered about here and there. The illustration (p. 60) represents a cluster of monument-like buildings which line the path and are dotted about in groups of from three to twelve or fourteen together. They stand about seven feet high and are, as the inhabitants of the village claim, erected over the defunct Lamas and other saints of the Buddhist religion, after which they become sacred in the eyes of the faithful, who refer to them with bowings and scrapings and "Om mani padme hums" innumerable.[3]

After some conversation, the monks invited M. Notovitch to

---

[3] "The Diary of a Pedestrian."

visit the convent, which invitation he at once accepted and followed them up the steep passages cut in the solid rock, which was thickly studded with prayer-wheels that are set twirling by the slightest touch, which is unavoidable in ascending the narrow passage.

He was conducted to a room, the walls of which were adorned with books, prayer-wheels and numerous statues of Buddha. He inquired about the manuscript relating to Issa, of which he had heard from the Lama of the Moulbek monastery. The monks here also denied having any of the rolls in their possession; one monk, however, acknowledged that he had seen many copies of the manuscript in a convent near Leh, where he had spent many years previous to his appointment to Lamieroo; but the visitor was unable to induce the monk to mention the name of the convent where the rolls were kept, and further questioning only provoked suspicion.

Europeans have not yet understood the reason why the monks and other custodians of the sacred literature of the East have been unwilling to give full information about manuscripts, although they would gladly explain the significance of other sacred objects; nor did M. Notovitch comprehend the reason for the refusal of the monks of Lamieroo to give him the desired information of the rolls relating to Jesus Christ.

In India, also, the European scholars and professors meet with the same difficulties. Dr. Peterson, Professor of Oriental Languages, met with a similar experience. There is a famous library of Jain manuscripts at Cambay, India. Dr. Peterson, in 1885, desiring to examine the manuscripts, made application to the custodians of the library, but was met with the most positive denial of the existence of any such library. Professor Roth, of Tubingen, wanted to know if there was a manuscript of the Atharva Veda in the Brahmin Library of Gwalior, but he was unable to obtain any information, although the political officer of that part of the country used his influence to put him in possession of a copy of the book. Dr. Bhandarkar, of the Deccan College, Poona, succeeded in examining only a few manuscripts of the Jain Libraries of Patan, and that only through the influence of the ruling prince, H. H. the Gaikwar of Baroda. Drs.

Buhler and Kielhorn, of Vienna and Leipsic, are under the fond impression that they have examined the whole collection of the Jain manuscripts at Jesalmer. But I know as a fact that the most important collection has never been shown to any foreigner. Europeans, as I said, have not been able to understand the reason why they are met with opposing obstacles in the search of ancient manuscripts. To me, however, in my official capacity as the Secretary of the Jain Association of India, the reason is simple enough. In the first place, the Mahomedan invaders of India burned our sacred manuscripts by hundreds and thousands; and, secondly, the first Christian missionaries who visited India possessed themselves of some of these manuscripts simply with a view to deride and belittle them, as it appears even in these days from the mass of rubbish which they have published in India on the religions of the people of that country. The Hindus and Jains, therefore, have always shown reluctance to part with their manuscripts.

Tibet, and especially Ladak, has had the same experience. A former ruler of Tibet, Langdar, otherwise called Langdharma, had tried to abolish the Buddhist doctrine in 900 A.C. He had commanded all temples and monasteries to be demolished, the images to be destroyed and the sacred books to be burnt. So intense was the indignation excited by these acts of sacrilege that he was murdered in the same year. In the sixteenth century, the historical books concerning Ladak were destroyed by the fanatical Mahomedans of Skardo who invaded the country, burned the monasteries, temples and religious monuments, and threw the contents of various libraries into the river Indus. Is it astonishing then that the Lama of the Lamieroo monastery should look with suspicions on the minute questioning of M. Notovitch?

From Lamieroo, M. Notovitch directed his attention towards Leh with the avowed determination of securing the manuscripts in question or go to Lassa. He therefore journeyed onward over difficult gorges, dangerous mountain passes, and through pleasant valleys, passing the celebrated fortress of Khalsi, dating from the time of the Mahomedan invasion, this being the only road leading from Kashmir to Tibet.

In crossing the valley Saspula and near the village of the same name, one sees two convents, on one of which our traveler was surprised to see floating a French flag, a present, he afterward learned, from a French engineer and used by the monks simply as a decoration.

M. Notovitch spent the night at the village and visited these convents where the monks took great delight in showing their visitor their books, rolls, images of Buddha, and the prayer-wheels, explaining politely and patiently all the sacred objects. Here, also, M. Notovitch received the same answers in reply to his inquiries, i.e., that the great monasteries alone possessed copies relating to the prophet Issa.

From here the traveler hastened on towards Leh, with no other object now than to secure a copy of the Buddhist records of the life of Jesus, which might perhaps, he thought, show the inner life of the best of men and complete the details so indistinct which the Scriptures give us about him.

On his arrival at Leh, M. Notovitch put up at the bungalow, specially built for Europeans who come over the Indian route in the hunting season.

Leh, the capital of Ladak, is a small town of five thousand inhabitants. It is built on pinnacles of rock. From a distance it has an imposing appearance which it owes entirely to the palace, built on a slight eminence, possessing a front of two hundred and fifty feet, and which is seven stories high. High above it, on the summit of a rocky mountain, is a monastery with its painted battlements and flags. In the centre of the town is a square, or market place, where merchants of India, China, Turkistan, Kashmir and Tibet, come to exchange their products for Tibetan gold.

The governor of Ladak, Vizier Surajbal, who has taken his degree as Doctor of Philosophy in London, resides in a vast two-storied building in the centre of the town. In honor of the foreign visitor he organized a polo game in the square, ending in the evening with dances and games in front of his terrace.

The following day M. Notovitch visited the famous Himis monastery, about twenty miles from Leh, situated on a high rock in the midst of the valley, overlooking the river Indus.

Himis is one of the principal monasteries of the country and contains a vast library of sacred works.

The entrance door is about six feet high, with steps leading up to it. The large massive doors painted with bright colors open into a court paved with pebbles. Inside is the principal temple containing a large statue of Buddha and other smaller statues. On the left is a veranda with an immense prayer-wheel on it; on the right there is a row of rooms for monks, all adorned with sacred paintings and small-prayer wheels.

The windows of the upper story, looking outward, have no panes of glass, but are closed by black curtains, upon which are sewn figures of a Latin cross, formed of white strips of cloth. The cross in different forms has been recognized as a mystic symbol by all ancient nations.

At the moment of his arrival M. Notovitch found all the Lamas of the convent, with their Lama-in-chief, formed in a circle around the great prayer-wheel. Underneath the veranda several musicians held drums and long trumpets. The whole company was anxiously awaiting in silence the commencement of a great religious mystery which was about to be presented. It is called a religious drama.

On certain days of the year religious dramas are performed by the Lamas, who call them Tambin Shi, "the bliss of instruction." Sometimes these dramas are performed by them in honor of distinguished visitors to their convent. Masked actors are introduced, who represent fantastically the various states of existence—spirits, men, animals, etc. This festival, with its singing, music and dancing, lasted for several hours. At the end, the Lama-in-chief invited the visitor to accompany him to the principal terrace, where they drank the chang of the festival (a kind of tasteless beer).

Regarding this religious festival, the Lama explained to the visitor that there was a religious side to all this theatrical performance which expressed to the initiate the fundamental principles of Buddhism, and was a practical means for maintaining the ignorant in obedience and love to the only Creator, just as a child is submissive to its parent by a plaything. These monasteries have several such festivals in a year, where the particulars are arranged by the Lamas to represent mysteries which have a great analogy to the pantomimes, where each actor executes almost all the movements and gestures he pleases in conforming himself to a principal idea. The mysteries of these pantomimes are nothing but a representation of the gods enjoying a general veneration—veneration which as a reward ought to give to man the happiness of conscience with which the idea of inevitable death and that of future life fill him.

Seizing upon the first moment which presented to broach the subject, M. Notovitch told the Lama that in a recent visit which he had made to a Gonpa,[4] one of the Lamas had spoken of a prophet Issa, and asked for further information.

The Lama replied: "The name of Issa is much respected among Buddhists, but he is scarcely known except among the chief Lamas, who have read the rolls relating to his life. There is an infinite number of Buddhas, similar to Issa, and the eighty-four thousand rolls which exist abound in details about each of them; but very few people have read a hundredth part of them. In order to conform to the established custom, each pupil or Lama who has visited Lassa does not fail to make a present of one or more of these copies to the convent to which he belongs. Our monastery possesses a great number of these, and among them are descriptions of the life and works of Buddha Issa, who preached the holy doctrines in India and among the sons of Israel, and who was put to death by the heathen whose descendants adopted the beliefs which he advocated, and these beliefs are yours. The great Buddha, the soul of the universe, is the incarnation of Brahma. He remains motionless most of the time, enclosing within himself all things since the origin of beings, and his breath gives life to the world. He has left man to his own will; at certain times, however, he throws off his inaction and invests himself with a human form in order to try and save his creatures from irremediable destruction. In the course of his terrestrial existence, Buddha creates a new world among the misled people; then he disappears again from the earth to become once

---

[4] Gonpa is a Tibetan name for a monastery.

more an invisible being, and return to his life of perfect felicity. Three thousand years ago the great Buddha incarnated himself into the celebrated Prince Shakya Muni, upholding and spreading abroad the doctrines of his twenty incarnations. Two thousand five hundred years ago the great soul of the world incarnated itself again in Gautama, casting the foundation of a new world in Burma, in Siam and in different islands. Soon afterwards Buddhism commenced to penetrate in China, thanks to the perseverance of the wise men who devoted themselves to propagate the holy doctrine, and under Ming-Ti, of the dynasty of Honi, about 2050 B.C., the doctrines of Shakya Muni received the adoption of the people. Simultaneously with the appearance of Buddhism in China, the doctrine commenced to spread itself among the Israelites. About 2,000 years ago the Perfect Being, still remaining in a state of inaction, incarnated himself in a new-born babe of a poor family. He willed that infant lips, by employing popular images, might enlighten the unfortunate people on the life beyond the grave, and might bring back men to the true path, by indicating to them by his own example the way which would best lead them to the original moral purity. When the holy child had reached a certain age he was taken to India, where, until he became a man, he studied all the laws of the great Buddha, whose everlasting dwelling is in heaven."

"The rolls brought from India to Nepal and from Nepal to Tibet, relating to the life of Issa, are written in the Pali language, and these are to be found at Lassa, but a copy in our language [Tibetan] exists here. The masses are, however, ignorant of Issa; there is scarcely any one but the great Lamas who know of him, because they have spent their entire lives studying these rolls which relate to Issa. But as his doctrine does not constitute a canonical part of Buddhism, and as the worshipers of Issa [Christians] do not recognize the authority of the Dalai Lama, in Tibet the prophet Issa is, like many of his kind, not recognized as one of their principal saints."

Here M. Notovitch inquired whether the act would be sinful, should be recite these copies to a stranger; the Lama replied: "That which belongs to God belongs also to men; duty obliges us to help with good grace the propagation of his doctrines;

only, I have no knowledge of where in our libraries these rolls are to be found; if you ever visit our Gonpa again it will be a pleasure to me to show them to you." Whereupon the Lama arose, saying that he was wanted for the sacrifices and asked kindly to be excused, and saluting the visitor, disappeared through the doorway.

There was nothing left for the somewhat disappointed traveler to do, but return to Leh and think out a plan which would furnish an excuse for returning to the convent. Two days later, he sent to the chief Lama a present consisting of an alarm-clock and a thermometer, with a message that he would probably pay a second visit to the convent before leaving Ladak and hoped that the Lama would favor him by showing him the rolls which had been the subject of their last conversation. M. Notovitch had formed the plan of leaving for Kashmir and again returning to Himis in order to allay any suspicion which might arise regarding his persistent inquiries concerning those rolls of the life of Issa. But fate decided the matter in his favor, for in passing along the mountain side, on the top of which stands the Gonpa of Pittak, his horse stumbled, by which our traveler was thrown to the ground and his leg broken. Not desiring to return to Leh, he ordered his porters to carry him to the Himis monastery, where he was received and kindly cared for.

M. Notovitch says: "In the morning I bandaged my leg with small oblong sticks which I tied together with a cord. I tried to make no superfluous movements; a favorable result was soon apparent; two days afterwards I was in a condition to leave the Gonpa and to undertake a slow journey towards India to find a doctor.

"While a young boy kept twirling all the time the prayer-wheel which was near my bed, the venerable old man who superintended the Gonpa entertained me with interesting stories; he often drew from their cases my alarm-clock and my watch asking me how to wind them up and what their use was. Acceding finally to my urgent requests he brought me two large bound books whose large leaves of paper had become yellow by time; he then read to me the biography of Issa which I wrote down carefully in my note-book according to the translation

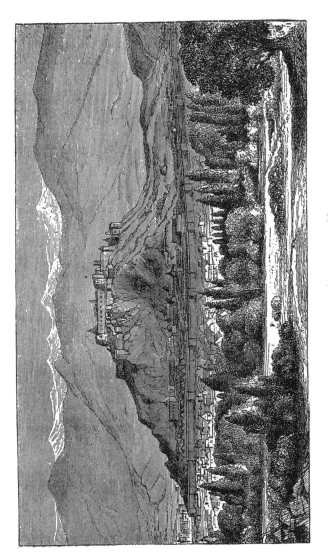

Hari Parvat (*See page 7.*)

which my interpreter made for me. This curious document is written in the form of isolated verses which very often have no connection with one another.

"The third day my health was so much improved that it allowed me to continue my journey. After having dressed my leg I turned back crossing Kashmir on my way to India. . . . I have long since desired to publish the life of Jesus Christ which I found at Himis and of which I have spoken above; but all kinds of business have completely taken up my time. It is only to-day after having spent long restless nights in arranging my notes, after having suitably grouped the verses in accordance with the narrative and impressed upon the whole the character of unity, that I resolved to publish THIS curious copy."

The Life of Saint Issa

THE BEST OF THE SONS OF MEN

I.

1. The earth trembled and the heavens wept because of the great crime just committed in the land of Israel.

2. For they have just finished torturing and executing there the great, just Issa in whom dwelt the soul of the universe,

3. Who incarnated himself in a simple mortal in order to do good to men and to exterminate evil thoughts,

4. And in order to bring back man degraded by sins to a life of peace, love and good, and to recall him to the only and indivisible Creator, whose mercy is infinite and boundless.

5. This is what the merchants, who came from Israel, relate on the subject.

II.

1. The people of Israel lived on a very fertile land, yielding two harvests a year, and possessed large flocks; they excited by their sins the wrath of God,

2. Who inflicted on them a terrible punishment, taking away their land, their flocks and their possessions. Israel was reduced to slavery by the powerful and rich Pharaohs who then reigned in Egypt.

3. The latter had made slaves of the Israelites and treated them worse than beasts, overloading them with heavy and difficult work and putting them in irons and covering their bodies with wounds and scars, denying them sufficient food and shelter.

4. This was in order to keep them in a state of continual fear and deprive them of all resemblance to human beings;

5. And in this great calamity the people of Israel, remembering their heavenly Protector, prayed and implored His grace and pity.

6. An illustrious Pharaoh reigned in Egypt at this time who rendered himself famous by his numerous victories and riches which he had accumulated and the large palaces which his slaves had erected with their own hands.

7. This Pharaoh had two sons, the younger of whom was called Mossa; the wise men of Israel taught him different sciences.

8. And they loved Mossa in Egypt for his kindness and for the compassion which he showed to all those who suffered.

9. Seeing that the Israelites would not, in spite of the intolerable sufferings which they endured, abandon their God to worship those which the hand of man had made and which were the gods of the Egyptians,

10. Mossa believed in their invisible God who did not allow their weakened forces to fail,

11. And the Israelite teachers excited the ardor of Mossa and implored him to intercede with Pharaoh his father, in favor of his co-religionists.

12. The Prince Mossa applied to his father imploring him to ameliorate the fate of the unfortunate people, but Pharaoh was enraged against him and only increased the torments of his slaves.

13. Shortly afterwards, a great misfortune visited Egypt;

the plague cut down the young and the old, the sick and the well, Pharaoh believed that his own gods were angry with him;

14. But Prince Mossa told his father that it was the God of the slaves who was interceding in favor of the unfortunates and was punishing the Egyptians;

15. Pharaoh then ordered Mossa to take all the slaves of the Jewish race and lead them out of the city, and to found at a great distance from the capital another city and there to live with them.

16. Mossa told the Hebrew slaves that he had freed them in the name of his God, the God of Israel; he departed with them from the city and from the land of Egypt.

17. He led them into the land which they had formerly lost by their many sins; he gave them laws and advised them always to pray to the invisible Creator whose kindness is infinite.

18. After the death of the Prince Mossa the Israelites observed his laws rigorously; God too recompensed them for the evils to which they had been subjected in Egypt.

19. Their kingdom became the most powerful in all the world, their kings became illustrious on account of their treasures and peace reigned long among the people of Israel.

III.

1. The fame of the riches of Israel was spread throughout the earth and the neighboring nations envied them.

2. But God led the victorious armies of the Hebrews and the heathen dared not attack them.

3. Unfortunately, man does not always obey his own better self, so the fidelity of the Israelites to their God did not long endure.

4. They soon forgot all the favors which He had heaped

upon them, and rarely invoked His name, but begged protection of the magicians and sorcerers;

5. The kings and captains submitted their own laws for those that Moses had left to them; the temples of God and the customs of worship were abandoned, and the people gave themselves up to pleasures and lost their original purity.

6. Several centuries had elapsed since their departure from Egypt, when God again thought of inflicting punishment on them.

7. Strangers began to invade the country of Israel, devastating the land, ruining the villages and forcing the inhabitants into captivity.

8. Heathens at one time came from beyond the seas from the country of Romulus; they subdued the Hebrews and appointed commanders of the army who governed them under the orders of Cæsar.

9. They destroyed the temples, compelling the people to sacrifice victims to the heathen gods instead of worshiping the invisible God.

10. Warriors were made of the nobles, the women were torn from their husbands; the lower class of the people, reduced to slavery, were sent by thousands across the sea.

11. As to the children they were killed by the sword, and throughout the whole country of Israel nothing but weeping and groaning was heard.

12. In their sore distress the people remembered again their great God; they implored His mercy and prayed Him to forgive them. Our Father in His inexhaustible kindness listened to their appeal.

IV.

1. The time had now come when the merciful Judge had chosen to incarnate Himself in a human being.

2. And the Eternal Spirit who remained in a condition of complete inaction and of supreme beatitude, aroused and detached Himself for an indefinite time from the Eternal Being,

3. In order to show, by assuming the human form, the means of identifying one's self with divinity and attaining eternal felicity;

4. And to show by His example how we may attain moral purity and separate the soul from its material envelope so that it may reach the perfection necessary to pass into the Kingdom of Heaven, which is unchangeable and where eternal happiness reigns.

5. Soon after, a wonderful child was born in the land of Israel; God Himself spoke by the mouth of this child of the insignificance of body, and the grandeur of soul.

6. The parents of this child were poor people, belonging by birth to a family distinguished for their piety, who had forgotten their ancient grandeur on earth, in celebrating the name of the Creator and thanking Him for the misfortunes with which He was pleased to try them.

7. To reward this family for remaining firm in the path of truth, God blessed their first-born child and elected him to go forth and uplift those that had fallen in evil and to cure those that were suffering.

8. The divine child, to whom they gave the name of Issa, began to speak, while yet a child, of the one indivisible God, exhorting the erring souls to repent and to purify themselves from those sins, of which they were guilty.

9. People came from all parts to listen to him and they marvelled at the words of wisdom which issued from his childish mouth; all the Israelites affirmed that in this child dwelt the Eternal Spirit.

10. When Issa reached the age of thirteen years, the time when an Israelite should take a wife,

11. The house where his parents earned a livelihood by means of modest labor, began to be a place of meeting for the rich and noble people who desired to have the young Issa for a son-in-law, who was already well-known by his edifying discourses in the name of the All-Powerful;

12. It was then that Issa disappeared secretly from his father's house, left Jerusalem, and with a caravan of merchants, went toward Sindh,

13. With the purpose of perfecting himself in the divine knowledge and of studying the laws of the great Buddhas.

V.

1. In the course of his fourteenth year, the young Issa, blessed of God, crossed the Sindh and established himself among the Aryas, in the cherished country of God.

2. The fame of this wonderful youth spread throughout Northern Sindh; when he crossed the country of the five rivers and Rajputana, the worshippers of the Jaina God implored him to dwell with them.

3. But he left them and went to Jagannath, in the country of Orissa, where lie the mortal remains of Vyasa-Krishna. Here the white priests of Brahma received him joyfully.

4. They taught him to read and understand the Vedas, to cure with the aid of prayers, to teach and explain the holy scriptures to the people, to drive away the evil spirit from the body of man, and to restore to him the human form.

5. He spent six years in Jagannath, Rajagriha, Benares and other holy cities. Every one loved Issa, for he lived in peace with the Vaishyas and Shudras, to whom he taught the holy scripture.

6. But the Brahmins and Kshatriyas said to him that the great Para-Brahma had forbidden them to approach those whom he had created from his belly and from his feet;

The Seventh Bridge of Shrinagar. (*See page 7.*)

7. That the Vaishyas were authorized to hear the reading of the Vedas only on the festival days,

8. That the Shudras were not only forbidden to attend the reading of the Vedas, but even to look at them; for their condition was to serve forever as slaves to the Brahmins, the Kshatriyas and even the Vaishyas;

9. "Death alone can free them from their servitude," Para-Brahma has said: "Leave them, therefore, and come and worship with us the gods that will be angry with you if you disobey them."

10. But Issa did not heed their words, and went among the Shudras to preach against the Brahmins and the Kshatriyas.

11. He strongly denounced the doctrine that gives to men the power of robbing their fellow-men of their human rights; in truth, he said: "God the Father has established no difference between his children, who are all equally dear to him."

12. Issa denied the divine origin of the Vedas and the Puranas, for he taught his followers that one law had been given to man to guide him in his actions:

13. "Fear thy God, bend thy knee only before Him, and bring to Him alone thy offerings which come from thy labors."

14. Issa denied the Trimurti and the incarnation of Para-Brahma in Vishnu, Shiva and other gods; for he said:

15. "The Eternal Judge, the Eternal Spirit composes the one individual soul of the universe, which alone creates, contains and vivifies the whole."

16. "It is He alone who has willed and created, who exists from eternity, whose existence will have no end; there is none equal to Him either in heaven or on earth."

17. "The great Creator has shared His power with no one, still less with inanimate objects, as they have taught you, for He alone possesses all power."

18. "He willed and the world appeared; by one divine

thought He united the waters and separated from them the dry part of the globe. He is the cause of the mysterious life of man, into whom He has breathed a part of His own."

19. "He has subordinated to man the land, the water, the beasts and all that He has created, and which He Himself preserves in an unchangeable order by fixing the proper duration of each."

20. "The anger of God will soon fall on man, for he has forgotten his Creator; he has filled His temples with abominations, and he adores numerous creatures which God has subordinated to him."

21. "For, in order to please stones and metals, he sacrifices human beings, in whom dwells a part of the spirit of God."

22. "For he humiliates those who toil by the sweat of their brow to gain the favor of the idle, who sit at sumptuously furnished tables."

23. "Those who deprive their brothers of the divine gift shall be deprived of it themselves, and the Brahmins and the Kshatriyas will become Shudras of the Shudras, with whom the Eternal will dwell forever."

24. "Because on the day of the last Judgment, the Shudras and the Vaishyas shall be pardoned on account of their ignorance; on the other hand, God will pour His wrath upon those who have arrogated His rights."

25. "The Vaishyas and the Shudras greatly admired these words of Issa, and begged him to teach them how to pray, so that they might secure their happiness."

26. He said to them: "Do not worship idols, for they do not hear you; do not listen to the Vedas, in which the truth is perverted; do not believe yourselves superior to others everywhere; do not humiliate your neighbor."

27. "Help the poor, sustain the feeble; do no evil to anyone; do not covet what others possess and you do not."

VI.

1. The white priests and the warriors having learnt of the discourse which Issa had addressed to the Shudras, determined upon his death, and with this intention sent their servants to search for the young prophet.

2. But Issa, warned of the danger by the Shudras, left Jagannath by night, reached the mountains, and established himself in the country of the Gautamides, where the great Buddha Shakya-Muni was born, amidst the people who worshiped the one and only sublime Brahma.

3. Having learned perfectly the Pali language, the just Issa devoted himself to the study of the sacred rolls of the Sutras.

4. Six years afterwards, Issa, whom the Buddha had chosen to spread the holy doctrine, was able to explain perfectly the sacred rolls.

5. Then he left Nepal and the Himalaya mountains, descended into the valley of Rajputana and journeyed toward the west, preaching to various peoples the possibility of man's attaining the supreme perfection,

6. And the good which each one should do to his neighbor, which is the surest means of being quickly absorbed into the Eternal Spirit; "he who had recovered his primitive purity," Issa said, "would die having obtained pardon for his sins, and the right to contemplate the majestic figure of God."

7. In traversing the heathen territories the divine Issa taught that the worship of visible gods was contrary to natural law.

8. "For man," he said, "has not been favored with the power to see the image of God and to construct a host of divinities resembling the Eternal One."

9. "Besides, it is incompatible with the human conscience to esteem the grandeur of divine purity less than animals or works executed by the hand of man in stone or metal."

10. "The Eternal Legislator is one infinite; there are no other gods but Him, He has not shared the world with anyone, nor has He informed anyone of His intentions."

11. "Just as a father would act toward his children, so shall God judge men after their death according to His merciful laws; never will He humiliate His child by making his soul migrate into the body of a beast as in purgatory."

12. "The celestial law," said the Creator through the mouth of Issa, "scorns the immolation of human beings to a statue or to an animal, for I have dedicated to the use of man all animals and all that the world contains."

13. "All has been given to man who is thus directly and intimately bound to me his Father; he who has taken away my child will be severely judged and chastised by the divine law."

14. "To the Eternal Judge man is nil, just as an animal is to a man."

15. "Therefore I say unto you, leave your idols, do not perform ceremonies that separate you from your Father, and link and bind you to priests against whom Heaven is turned."

16. "For it is they who have led you astray from the true God and whose superstitions and cruelty are leading you to the perversion of spirit and to the loss of all moral sense."

VII.

1. The words of Issa were spread abroad among the heathen in the countries through which he traveled and the people abandoned their idols.

2. Seeing this the priests demanded from him who glorified the name of the true God, proofs of the reproaches that he had heaped upon them and the demonstration of the powerlessness of their idols, in the presence of the people.

3. And Issa replied to them: "If your idols and animals are powerful and really possess a supernatural power, let them annihilate me on the spot."

4. "Perform a miracle," the priests answered him, "and let thy God confound ours if they inspire him with disgust."

5. But Issa answered: "The miracles of our God began with the creation of the universe, they take place now every day, every moment, and whosoever does not see them is deprived of one of the most beautiful gifts of life."

6. "And it is not upon pieces of inanimate stone or metal or wood that the anger of God will fall, but it will fall upon men, who must for their own safety destroy all the idols which they have made:"

7. "Just as a stone and grain of sand which are as nothing before men, wait with resignation the time when he will utilize and make of them something useful and beautiful,"

8. "Just so man must wait for the great favor which God will accord him in honoring him with a decision."

9. "But alas for you, opponents of men! if it is not the favor but the wrath of Divinity that you await; woe unto you if you wait for Him to show His power by miracles!"

10. "For it is not the idols which He shall destroy in His wrath, but those who have erected them; their hearts shall be a prey to an eternal fire and their lacerated bodies will be given to satisfy the appetite of wild beasts."

11. "God will expel the contaminated animals from His flocks but He will take back to Himself those who were misled by having misunderstood the celestial spark which dwelt in them."

12. Seeing the powerlessness of their priests these people believed in the teachings of Issa and adopted his faith and in fear of the anger of the Divinity broke their idols in pieces; seeing this the priests fled to escape the popular vengeance.

13. And Issa taught the heathen not to try to see the

The carriers of M. Notovitch (*See page 9.*)

Eternal Spirit with their own eyes, but rather to feel it with their heart and by a soul truly pure render themselves worthy of His favors.

14. He said to them: "Not only must you desist from making human sacrifices, but in general from sacrificing any animal to which life has been given, for all that has been created is for the benefit of man."

15. "Steal not the property of another, for this would be taking away from your neighbor the things which he has acquired by the sweat of his brow."

16. "Deceive not any one, thus you shall not be deceived yourselves; try to justify yourselves before the last judgment, for then it will be too late."

17. "Do not give yourselves up to debauchery, for that is violating the laws of God."

18. "Supreme happiness shall be attained not only by purifying yourselves, but also by guiding others in the way which will achieve for them the primitive perfection."

VIII.

1. The neighboring countries were filled with the renown of the teachings of Issa, and when he entered Persia the priests became alarmed and forbade the people to listen to him.

2. But when they saw all the villages greeting him with joy and piously listening to his sermons, they caused him to be arrested and brought before the high priest where he was submitted to the following questions.

3. "Of what new God dost thou teach? Dost thou not know, unfortunate one that thou art, that the holy Zoroaster is the only just man admitted to the honor of receiving communications from the Supreme Being?"

4. "He has ordered the angels to record in writing the

words of God for the use of his people—the laws that were given to Zoroaster in paradise."

5. "Who then art thou that darest to blaspheme our God and sow doubt in the hearts of believers?"

6. And Issa said unto them: "I do not speak of a new God, but of our Heavenly Father who existed before the beginning and who will exist after the eternal end."

7. "It is of Him that I have taught the people, who like an innocent child cannot yet understand God by the only force of their intelligence and penetrate His divine and spiritual sublimity."

8. "But as a new-born child recognizes in the dark its mother's breast, just so your people who have been led in error by your erroneous doctrine and religious ceremonies have recognized instinctively their Father in the God, of whom I am the prophet."

9. "The Eternal Being says to your people through the medium of my mouth: 'You should not worship the sun for it is only a part of the world which I have created for man.'"

10. "'The sun rises in order to warm you during your labors; it sets so as to give you rest which I have fixed.'"

11. "'It is only to me and to me alone that you owe all that you possess, all that surrounds you, either above or below.'"

12. "But," began the priests, "how could a people live according to the laws of justice, if they had no teachers?"

13. Issa answered: "As long as the people had no priests, they were governed by natural laws and preserved the candour of their souls."

14. "Their souls were in God and when they wanted to communicate with the Father they did not have recourse to the mediation of an idol, an animal or a fire as you practise here."

15. "You pretend that one must worship the sun, the spirit of good and of evil; well, I say to you that your doctrine is detestable. The sun does not act spontaneously, but by the will of the invisible God who has created it."

16. "And who has willed that this star should light the day and should warm the labor and the crops of man."

17. "The eternal spirit is the soul of all that it animates. You commit a great sin in dividing Him into the spirit of evil and that of good, for there is no God except that of good."

18. "Who like unto the father of a family does only good to his children, whose faults he forgives if they repent of them."

19. "And the evil spirit dwells upon the earth in the heart of those men who turn the children of God from the right path."

20. "Therefore I say unto you: Fear the judgment day for God will inflict a terrible punishment upon those who have forced His children to deviate from the true light and who have filled them with superstition and prejudice,"

21. "Upon those who have blinded the seeing, carried contagion to the strong, and taught the worship of those things which God has given to man for his own good and to aid him in his labors."

22. "Your doctrine is therefore the fruit of your error, for in desiring to approach the God of truth you have created for yourselves false gods."

23. After having listened to him the priests resolved to do no evil to him, but during the night while all in the city slept, they led him outside the walls and there left him to his fate upon the highway in the hope that he would soon become the prey of wild beasts.

24. But protected by our God, Saint Issa continued his way unharmed.

IX.

1. Issa, whom the Creator had chosen to bring back the true God to men plunged in sin, was twenty-nine years old when he arrived in the land of Israel.

2. Since the departure of Issa the heathen had caused the Israelites to endure still more atrocious sufferings, and they were now a prey to the greatest despair.

3. Many among them had already abandoned the laws of their God and those of Moses, hoping to soften their fierce conquerors.

4. In the presence of this situation Issa exhorted his countrymen not to despair because the day of redemption of sins was near, and he strengthened their belief in the God of their fathers.

5. "Children, do not give yourselves up to despair," said the Heavenly Father by the mouth of Issa, "for I have heard your voice and your cries have reached even unto me."

6. "Do not weep, O my beloved, for your cries have touched the heart of your Heavenly Father, and He has forgiven you as He forgave your ancestors."

7. "Do not forsake your family to plunge yourselves into iniquity, lose not the nobility of your feelings, and worship not idols which will remain deaf to your voice."

8. "Fill my temple with your hope and your patience and do not abjure the religion of your fathers, for I alone have guided them and heaped favors on them."

9. "You shall raise those who have fallen, you shall give food to those that are hungry, and you shall help the sick that you may be pure and just at the day of judgment which I am preparing for you."

10. The Israelites came in throngs to hear the words of Issa, and asked him where they should praise their Heavenly Father, since the enemy had razed their temples to the ground and lain profane hands on their sacred vessels.

11. Issa answered them that God had no reference to temples built by the hand of man, but that He meant the hearts of men which are the true temples of God.

12. "Enter into your temple, into your heart, enlighten it with good thoughts, with patience and with firm confidence which you should place in your Father."

13. "And your sacred vessels, these are your heads and eyes; see and do that which is pleasing to God, for in doing good to your neighbor you perform a ceremony which beautifies the temple where He lives who has given you life."

14. "For God has created you in His own image innocent, with the soul pure, the heart filled with kindness, and not intended for the conception of evil schemes, but made to be the sanctuary of love and justice."

15. "Do not therefore defile your heart, I say unto you, for the Eternal Being dwells there always."

16. "If you wish to accomplish works of piety or love, do them with an open heart and let not your action be governed by hope of gain or mercenary thoughts."

17. "For these actions will not bring you salvation and you will then fall into a state of moral degradation where lying, theft and assassination pass as generous deeds."

X.

1. Holy Issa went from one city to another, confirming with the word of God the courage of the Israelites who were ready to succumb under the weight of despair, and thousands of men followed to hear his teachings.

The shaky bridge of Kashmir (*See page* 9.)

2. But the rulers of the cities feared him and informed the principal Governor who dwelt at Jerusalem that a man called Issa had arrived in the country, that by his sermons he was rousing the people against the authorities, that the multitude listened to him eagerly and neglected the works of the state, stating that in a short time it would be rid of its ruling intruders.

3. Then Pilate, the governor of Jerusalem, ordered them to seize the person of the preacher Issa, bring him into the city and lead him before the judges; but so as to not excite discontent among the people, Pilate ordered the priests and the wise men, aged Hebrews, to judge him in the temple.

4. Meanwhile, Issa continuing his preaching came to Jerusalem; having learned of his arrival, all the inhabitants who knew him already by reputation went to meet and greet him.

5. They saluted him respectfully and opened the doors of their temple to him in order to hear from his lips what he had said in the other towns of Israel.

6. And Issa said unto them: "The human race is perishing because of its lack of faith, for the darkness and the tempest have confused the flock of mankind and they have lost their shepherd."

7. "But the tempest will not last forever, the darkness will not hide the light forever, the heavens will soon become serene, the heavenly brightness will soon spread over the whole earth and the wandering flocks will gather themselves around their shepherd."

8. "Do not try to seek for the direct roads in darkness for fear of falling in a ditch, but gather together your lost forces, aid each other, place all your confidence in your God and wait till the first light appears."

9. "He who aids his neighbor aids himself and whoever protects his own family protects his people and his country."

10. "For be sure that the day is near when you will be

delivered from darkness; you shall gather yourselves together in one family and your enemy who ignores the favor of the great God shall tremble in fear."

11. The priests and the elders who listened to him, full of wonder at his words, asked him if it was true that he had tried to arouse the people against the authorities of the country as had been reported to Governor Pilate.

12. "Can one rise against misled men to whom darkness has hidden the way and the door?" answered Issa. "I have only warned the unfortunate as I do here in this temple so that they may not advance further on dark roads, for an abyss is open at their feet."

13. "Earthly power is not of long duration and it is subject to many changes. It would be of no use for a man to revolt against it, for one power always succeeds another and it will thus be until the extinction of humanity."

14. "On the contrary do you not see that the powerful and the rich sow among the sons of Israel a spirit of rebellion against the eternal power of Heaven?"

15. And then the elders said: "Who art thou and from what country art thou come even unto us? Heretofore we have not heard thee spoken of, and we are even ignorant of thy name."

16. "I am an Israelite," answered Issa, "and on the day of my birth I saw the walls of Jerusalem, and heard the wailings of my brothers reduced to slavery and the lamentations of my sisters carried away among the heathen."

17. "And my soul was painfully grieved when I saw that my brothers had forgotten the true God; while yet a child I left my father's house to go and settle among other nations."

18. "But hearing that my brothers suffered still greater tortures I returned to the country where my parents dwelt, to recall my brothers to the faith of their ancestors, which teaches us patience upon earth so that we may obtain perfect and sublime happiness above."

19. And the learned elders asked him this question: "They claim that thou deniest the laws of Mossa and that thou teachest the people to abandon the temple of God?"

20. And Issa answered: "We do not demolish what has been given by our heavenly Father and what has been destroyed by sinners, but I have advised them to purify their heart of every stain, for *there* is the true temple of God."

21. "As for the laws of Mossa I have tried to re-establish them in the heart of men, but I tell you that you do not understand their true meaning, for it is not vengeance, but pardon that they teach; only the sense of these laws has been perverted."

XI.

1. Having heard Issa, the priests and the learned elders decided among themselves not to judge him for he did no evil to anyone, and presenting themselves before Pilate, the Governor of Jerusalem, chosen by the heathen King of the country of Romulus, they addressed him thus:

2. "We have seen the man whom thou accusest of exciting our people to revolt, we have heard his teachings and we know that he is our fellow-countryman."

3. "But the rulers of the towns have sent thee false reports, for he is a just man who teaches the people the word of God. After having questioned him we let him go in peace."

4. The Governor became violently enraged and sent his servants in disguise to spy after Issa and to report to the authorities every word that he addressed to the people.

5. The holy Issa continued, however, to visit the neighboring towns and preach the true ways of the Creator, exhorting the Hebrews to patience and promising them a speedy deliverance.

6. During all this time many people followed him wherever he went; many did not quit him, but they served him as servants.

7. And Issa said: "Do not believe in miracles performed by the hand of man, for He who commands nature is alone able to perform supernatural things, while man is powerless to soften the rage of winds and to distribute rain."

8. "There is one miracle, however, that it is possible for man to perform; it is, when full of sincere belief, he decides to uproot from his heart all bad thoughts, and to attain this end, he goes no more into the paths of evil."

9. "And all the things which are done without God are but great errors, seductions and enchantments, which show only how far the soul of him who practices this art is full of shamelessness, falsehood and impurity,"

10. "Put no faith in oracles, for God alone knows the future; he who has recourse to sorcerers, defiles the temple which is in his heart and shows distrust for his Creator."

11. "Faith in sorcerers and their oracles destroys the innate simplicity in man and his child-like purity; an infernal power takes possession of him and forces him to commit all sorts of crimes and worship idols;"

12. "While the Lord, our God, who has no equal, is one, all-powerful, all-knowing and present everywhere; it is He who alone possesses all wisdom and all light."

13. "It is to Him that you must pray for being comforted in your griefs, aided in your works, cured in your sickness; whoever will have recourse to Him will not suffer refusal."

14. "The secret of nature is in the hands of God, for the world, before it appeared, existed in the depths of the Divine thought; it has become material and visible by the will of the Most High."

15. "When you would seek Him, become children, for you

know neither the past, nor the present nor the future and God is master of time."

XII.

1. "Just man!" said the disguised servants of the Governor of Jerusalem, "tell us whether we should execute the will of our Cæsar or await our near deliverance."

2. And Issa having recognized in the questioners the people bribed to follow him, said to them: "I have not said that you would be delivered from Cæsar; it is the soul which is plunged into error that will have deliverance."

3. "There can be no family without a head and there can be no order among a people without a Cæsar whom they must obey blindly, for he alone shall answer for his acts before the supreme tribunal."

4. "Does Cæsar possess a divine right," the spies again asked, "and is he the best of mortals?"

5. "There is none best among men, but truly there are some that are sick whom chosen men charged with this mission should care for, by using the means which the sacred law of our Heavenly Father confers upon them."

6. "Clemency and justice are the highest gifts granted to Cæsar, his name will be illustrious if he holds to them."

7. "But he who acts otherwise, who transgresses the limits of his power over those under his rule, endangering their life, offends the great Judge and wrongs His dignity in the opinion of men."

8. Meanwhile an old woman who had approached the crowd to hear Issa better was pushed aside by one of the disguised men who placed himself before her.

9. Issa then said: "It is not good for a son to push aside his mother so that he may occupy the front place which should be

Scene near Surghol (*See page 10.*)

hers. Whoever does not respect his mother, the most sacred being after God, is unworthy of the name of son."

10. "Listen to these words: Respect woman for she is the mother of the universe and the truth of divine creation lies within her."

11. "She is the foundation of all that is good and beautiful, as also the germ of life and death. Upon her depends the whole life of man for she is his moral and natural support in his labors."

12. "She gives birth to you amid suffering; by the sweat of her brow she attends your growth and until her death you cause her the greatest anxiety. Bless her and adore her, for she is your only friend and support upon earth."

13. "Respect and defend her; in acting thus you will win her love and her heart, and you will please God, and many of your sins will be forgiven."

14. "Therefore, love your wives and respect them, for they will be mothers to-morrow, and later elders of a whole nation."

15. "Be submissive to your wife; her love ennobles a man, softens his hardened heart, tames the beast and makes a lamb of it."

16. "Wife and mother are inestimable treasures bestowed of God; they are the most beautiful ornaments of the universe, and of them will be born all who shall inhabit the world."

17. "Just as the God of armies formerly separated the light from darkness and the land from waters, so woman possesses the divine talent to separate the good from evil intentions in man."

18. "Therefore I say unto you, after God your best thoughts should belong unto women and to your wives; she is the divine temple where you will obtain easily perfect happiness."

19. "Draw from this temple your moral force; there you will forget your troubles and your failures; there you will recover your wasted forces which are necessary in helping your neighbors."

20. "Do not expose her to humiliations, for thereby you humiliate yourself and lose the sentiment of love, without which nothing exists here below."

21. "Protect your wife that she may protect you and all your family; all that you will do for your mother, your wife, for a widow or another woman in distress, you shall have done for your God."

XIII.

1. Holy Issa thus taught the people of Israel for three years in every town and village, on the highways and on the plains, and all that he predicted was realized.

2. During all this time the disguised servants of the Governor Pilate observed him closely without hearing anything resembling the reports formerly made against Issa by the rulers of the towns.

3. But the Governor Pilate, fearing the great popularity of the Saint Issa, whom his opponents believed to be inciting the people to have himself chosen for king, ordered one of his spies to accuse him.

4. Then he ordered the soldiers to proceed to arrest him, and they imprisoned him in a dungeon, where they caused him to endure various torments, hoping thereby to force him to accuse himself, which would permit them to put him to death.

5. The Saint, desiring only the perfect happiness of his brothers, endured these torments in the name of his Creator.

6. The servants of Pilate continued torturing him, reducing him to a state of extreme weakness; but God was with him and did not suffer him to die.

7. Learning of the sufferings and tortures which their Saint endured, the principal priests and wise elders requested the Governor to set Issa free on the occasion of a great feast which was near at hand.

8. But the Governor refused them decidedly. They asked him then to have Issa appear before the tribunal of the elders in order that he might be condemned or acquitted before the feast; Pilate consented to this.

9. The next day the Governor called together the principal captains, priests, wise elders and legislators for the purpose of having them judge Issa.

10. They brought the Saint from his prison, and seated him before the Governor between two robbers, who were then on trial, and to show the people that he was not the only one to be condemned.

11. And Pilate, addressing Issa, said: "O man! is it true that thou dost incite the people against the authorities with the intention of becoming the king of Israel thyself?"

12. "One does not become king by his own will," answered Issa, "and they have spoken falsely to you in asserting that I was inciting the people. I have never spoken but of the King of Heaven, and it is He whom I taught the people to worship."

13. "For the sons of Israel have lost their original purity, and if they do not have recourse to the true God they will be sacrificed and their temple will fall in ruin."

14. "Temporal power maintains order in a country; I have therefore taught them not to forget it; I said to them: 'Live according to your position and fortune, so as not to disturb public order;' and I exhorted them also to remember that disorder reigned in their heart and in their soul."

15. "Thus the King of Heaven has punished them and suppressed their national kings. Nevertheless I said to them: 'If you resign yourselves to your fate, the Kingdom of Heaven will be reserved to you as a reward.'"

16. At this moment the witnesses were introduced, one of whom testified, saying: "Thou hast taught the people that the temporal power was nothing before that of the king who would soon free the Israelites from the heathen yoke."

17. "Blessed be thou," said Issa, "for having told the truth; the King of Heaven is greater and more powerful than terrestrial law, and His Kingdom surpasses all kingdoms here below."

18. "And the time is not far distant when conformably to the Divine will, the people of Israel shall purify themselves of their sins, for it is said that a precursor shall come and announce the deliverance of the people and unite them in one family."

19. And the Governor addressing the judges, said: "Do you hear this? The Israelite Issa acknowledges the crime of which he is accused. Judge him then according to your laws and pronounce upon him capital punishment."

20. "We cannot condemn him;" answered the priests and the elders, "thou hast thyself heard that he alluded to the King of Heaven, and that he has preached nothing which constitutes insubordination against our laws."

21. The Governor then summoned the witness who at the instigation of his master, Pilate, had betrayed Issa; this man came and addressing Issa, said: "Didst thou not make thyself pass as king of Israel when thou didst say that He who reigns in Heaven had sent thee to prepare His people?"

22. And Issa having blessed him, said: "Thou shalt be forgiven, for what thou sayest cometh not from thee." Then addressing the Governor he said: "Why humiliate thy dignity and teach thy inferiors to live in falsehood, since even without this thou hast the power to condemn an innocent person?"

23. At these words the Governor became violently enraged and ordered Issa to be condemned to death and the two robbers to be acquitted.

24. The judges having consulted together, said to Pilate:

"We will not take upon ourselves the great sin of condemning an innocent man, and of acquitting robbers, which is contrary to our laws."

25. "Do, therefore, as thou pleaseth." Having said this the priests and the wise men went out and washed their hands in a sacred vessel, saying: "We are innocent of the death of this just man."

XIV.

1. By order of the Governor the soldiers seized Issa and the two robbers and led them to a place of punishment and there nailed them upon crosses which they erected.

2. All day long the bodies of Issa and the two robbers remained suspended dripping with blood, under the guard of the soldiers; the people stood round about them, the relatives of the tortured praying and weeping.

3. At sunset the suffering of Issa ended. He lost his consciousness and the soul of this just man freed itself from his body to be absorbed in the Divinity.

4. Thus ended the terrestial life of the reflection of the Eternal Spirit in the form of a man who endured so much suffering, saving hardened sinners.

5. Pilate, however, through his own actions feared the throng, and returned the body of the Saint to his relatives, who interred it near the place of execution; the people came to pray at his tomb filling the air with weeping and wailings.

6. Three days afterwards fearing a general uprising, the Governor sent soldiers to raise secretly the body of Issa and bury it in some other place.

7. The next day the throng found the tomb open and empty; so that the rumor was spread that the Supreme Judge had sent His angels to carry away the mortal remains of the Saint in whom had dwelt on earth a part of the Divine Spirit.

A Buddhist monastery in Ladak (*See page 15.*)

8. When the rumor reached Pilate he was very angry and forbade them under penalty of slavery and death ever to utter the name of Issa, or to pray to the Lord for him.

9. But the people continued to weep and to glorify their Master aloud; so that many of them were led into captivity and subjected to torture and put to death.

10. Then many of the disciples of the Holy Issa left the country of Israel and went among the heathen, preaching that they must abandon their errors and think of the safety of their souls and the perfect happiness awaiting human beings in the immaterial world of light and wisdom wherein reposes in all His purity and perfect majesty, the great Creator.

11. The heathen, their kings and their warriors, listened to these preachers, abandoned their absurd beliefs, left their priests and their idols to celebrate the praises of the very wise Creator of the Universe, the King of Kings, whose heart is filled with infinite mercy.

Summary

In reading the preceding story of the life of Issa (Jesus Christ) we are on the one hand struck by the resemblance between some of its principal passages and the biblical and evangelical story and on the other hand by the contradictions equally remarkable which often differentiate the Buddhist version from the Old and New Testaments.

To explain this singularity it is necessary to take into account the times when these facts were consigned to writing.

We have been taught, it is true, since our childhood that the Pentateuch was written by Moses, but the careful investigation of contemporary scholars have shown conclusively that in the days of Moses and even long after him there existed no writing in those countries whose shores were washed by the Mediterranean, except the Egyptian hieroglyphics and the cuneiform inscriptions which are still found in the ruins of Babylon. But we know, on the contrary, that the alphabet and parchment were known in China and India long before Moses. Of this we have sufficient proofs.

The sacred books of "The Religion of Savants" teach us that the alphabet was invented in China in 2800 B.C., by Fou-si, who was the first emperor of China to adopt this religion; it was he who arranged its ritual and external ceremonies. Yao, the fourth of the Chinese emperors who belonged to this faith, published the moral and civil laws and in 2228 B.C. he framed a penal code. The fifth emperor, Soune, proclaimed in the year of his accession to the throne that the Religion of Savants would thenceforth be the religion of the State and in 2282 B.C., he enacted new penal laws. His laws, modified by the Emperor Woo Wang, founder of the Chow dynasty in 1122, are really known under the name of "Changes."

On the other hand, the doctrine of Buddha Fo whose true name was Shakya Muni, was written on parchment. Foism began to spread in China about 260 B.C.; in 206 an emperor of the Tsine dynasty desirous of studying Buddhism had invited a Buddhist named Silifan from India, and the Emperor Ming-Ti of the Hane dynasty, a year before the birth of Jesus Christ, procured from India the sacred books written by the Buddha Shakya Muni, founder of the Buddhist doctrine, who lived about 1200 years before Jesus Christ.

The doctrine of Buddha Gautama or Gotama, who lived 600 years B.C., was written on parchment in the Pali language. At this time, there existed already in India, about 84,000 Buddhist manuscripts which had been compiled for a great number of years.[1]

While the Chinese and the Hindus possessed already a very rich written literature, among less fortunate or more ignorant people who had no alphabet, accounts were transmitted orally from generation to generation. Owing to the untrustworthiness of the human memory and its relative incapacity, with Oriental fancy added to it, the historical facts soon degenerated into fabulous legends which later on, were collected together by the unknown compilers and given to the world under the name of the "Five Books of Moses;" legend also attributes to the Hebrew law-giver an extraordinary divine power and credits him with a series of miracles performed in the presence of Pharaoh; it has even been mistaken in declaring that he was an Israelite by birth.

The Hindu chroniclers, on the contrary, thanks to the invention of the alphabet, have been able to preserve not legends, but

---

[1] Buddha Shakya Muni and Buddha Gautama are really the same. But the Buddhists believe that many other Buddhas preceded the Buddha who lived 600 years before Jesus. As to the year when the Buddha Shakya Muni died, the Buddhists books differ considerably—the most distant periods mentioned being the years 2422 and 544 B.C.—Translator.

the accounts of deeds recently performed or the reports of merchants who had just returned after visiting foreign countries.

It should be remembered here, that in ancient as well as in
our own times, all the public life of the Orient was concentrated
in the bazaars where the news from foreign countries were
propagated by caravans of merchants who were usually followed
by dervishes whose business it was to recite new events in public places and temples and thus obtain a living. Soon after their
return from a journey or from business the merchants related all
that they had seen or heard.[2]

The commerce of India with Egypt and afterwards with
Europe passed through Jerusalem, where even in the time of
King Solomon, Hindu caravans brought precious metals and all
materials for the construction of temples. Merchandise from
Europe arrived at Jerusalem by sea and was unloaded in a har-
bor which is now the site of Jaffa.[3]

The chronicles in question were written before, during and
after Jesus Christ; but during his sojourn in India, where he
went as a mere pilgrim to study the Brahmin and Buddhist laws,
no special attention was given him. But later, when the first
reports of these events in Israel reached India, the chroniclers
after having consigned to writing all they had heard about the
prophet Issa whom an oppressed race had followed and who by
order of Pilate had been put to death, remembered that this
same Issa of Israelite origin had recently lived and studied
among them and then returned to his own country. Soon an
interest was created for this man who had so rapidly grown in
importance in their eyes and they immediately began to inquire
about his birth, his death and all the details of his life.

The two manuscripts read to me by the Lama of the Himis
monastery were collections of different copies written in the

---

[2] From very ancient times it has been a very common practice in the Orient for
the pilgrims and travelers to compose in verses the description of the places
they visit and the recital of events that impress them; and these little poems
are committed to memory and often recited by the people. There are numerous such poems among the Jains.—Translator.

[3] I have proved the antiquity of the Indian trade in my Introduction.—
Translator.

Tibetan language—translations of some rolls belonging to the Library of Lassa and brought from India, Nepal and Magadha, about 200 years after Christ, to a convent standing on Mount Marbour near Lassa where the Dalai Lama now resides.

These rolls were written in the Pali language which certain Lamas study in order to be able to translate into the Tibetan dialect.

The chroniclers were Buddhists belonging to the sect of Buddha Gotama. The references relating to Jesus in these chronicles are not put in order but are mixed up without sequence or coherence so far as contemporary events are concerned.

The manuscript begins without explanation or detail the accounts as they were given by some merchants who came from Judea in the year of the death of Jesus, that a just man by the name of Issa, an Israelite, after having been twice acquitted by the judges as being the man of God, was nevertheless put to death by the order of the heathen Governor Pilate, who feared that Jesus would, by his great popularity, be able to re-establish the Kingdom of Israel and expel those who had conquered it.

Finally communications just as incoherent came to us about the teachings of Jesus among the Guebres and other heathens. These reports seem to have been brought in the first year that followed the death of Jesus in whom they took an interest still greater.

One of the accounts given by a merchant speaks of the origin of Jesus and his family; another relates the expulsion of his partisans and the persecutions which they endured.

It is only at the end of the second volume that we find the first categorical affirmation of the chronicler where he says that Issa is blessed by God and that he is the best of all men, that he is the one in whom the great Brahma had chosen to incarnate His spirit which is separated from the Supreme Being at a period fixed by fate.

After having said that Issa descended from poor parents of Israelite origin, the chronicler digresses a little with the intention of explaining, according to old narrations, who the sons of Israel were. I have arranged all the fragments concerning the life of Issa in chronological order, and I have tried to give them the character of unity which they totally lacked.

I leave to scholars, philosophers and theologians the task of searching for the causes of the contradictions that may be found between this version of the life of Issa which I deliver to the public and the accounts of the Evangelists, but I believe no one will hesitate to agree with me that the version which I present to the public recorded three or four years after the death of Jesus, according to the statement of eye-witnesses and contemporaries, is more likely to be authentic than the accounts of the Evangelists who wrote at different times and so long after the actual occurrence of the events, that there is no wonder if the facts are misconstrued or the sense is altered.

Before touching on the life of Jesus, I must say a few words upon the history of Moses, who according to the most accredited belief was an Israelite. This is contradicted by the Buddhist records from which we learn that Moses was a prince of Egypt, the son of a Pharaoh and that the Israelite scholars were employed merely as his teachers. By carefully examining this important point we must admit that the Buddhist authors were right.

Having no desire to destroy the biblical legend concerning the origin of Moses, I believe that many will admit with me that Moses was not a simple Israelite, for this appreciable reason, that the education which he had received was that of the son of a king, and it is therefore difficult to believe that a child brought by mere chance into the palace should have been placed on equal standing with the son of the ruling sovereign (and that his education should have been considered of like importance). The manner in which the Egyptians treated their slaves shows that they were not particularly distinguished for generosity of character. A foundling (the child of a slave) would certainly not have been placed with the children of Pharaoh but would have been placed with his servants. Add to this the fact (and this is preponderating evidence) that the spirit of caste was so strictly observed in ancient Egypt.

On the other hand it is impossible to doubt that Moses had received a complete education; without that how could we

Lamieroo (*See page 13.*)

explain his great work of legislation, his large views and his high qualities as a ruler?

But if he was a prince, why was he attached to the Israelites? The explanation seems very simple to me. We know that among the ancients, as in our modern times, contentions existed between brothers as to who should succeed their father on the throne. Why not admit this hypothesis that Moses had dreams of founding a distinct kingdom, the fact that he had an elder brother preventing him from entertaining any hope of ever coming to the throne of Egypt? It was perhaps with this object that he attached himself to the Israelites whom he admired for their firmness in their belief and their bodily strength. We know that the Israelites of Egypt did not at all resemble their descendants physically; the blocks of granite used in building the palaces and pyramids stand there as evidence of this.

I explain in the same manner the history of the miracles which Moses might have performed before Pharaoh. Without bringing definite arguments for denying the miracles performed before Pharaoh in the name of God, you will agree, I think without much difficulty, that the Buddhist version is more probable than the biblical interpretation. The small-pox, plague or cholera must have caused enormous ravages in such an intensely dense population at a time when ideas upon hygiene were still rudimentary and when consequently the disease must have assumed fearful proportions.

Moses, whose intelligence was quick and prompt to show itself, was well able to work on the fears evinced by Pharaoh before the unchained elements, by explaining to him that it was due to the intervention of the God of Israel in favor of his chosen people.

This was the most opportune moment for Moses to deliver the children of Israel from bondage and of bringing them under his own domination.

Conformable to the will of Pharaoh, still according to the Buddhists, Moses led the Israelites beyond the walls of the city; but instead of building a new city near the capital as he had been ordered by Pharaoh, he led them out of the Egyptian territory. One can easily understand the indignation of Pharaoh upon learning that Moses infringed upon his commands, so he ordered his soldiers to pursue the fugitives. It seems, from the geographical situation of this region, that Moses must have skirted the mountain in his route and entered Arabia by the Isthmus now cut by the Suez Canal. Pharaoh, on the contrary, led his troops in a direct line towards the Red Sea, and in order to overtake the Israelites, who had already reached the opposite shore, he wanted to take advantage of the ebb of the sea into the gulf, formed by the shores and the isthmus and make his soldiers ford it. But the distance across the arm of the sea at this point was greater than he anticipated, for the tide closed in on the Egyptian army when they were half way across and none of them could possibly escape death.

This fact, so simple in itself, was transformed after centuries into a religious legend among the Israelites, who saw in it a divine intervention as a punishment inflicted by their God upon their enemies. We think that Moses himself entertained this belief. But that is a thesis which I will undertake to develop in a future work.

The Buddhist chronicle then describes briefly the greatness and the downfall of the kingdom of Israel and its conquest by strangers, who reduced its people to a state of servitude.

The misfortunes which befell the Israelites and their bitter afflictions henceforth were, according to the chronicler, reasons more than sufficient for God to take pity on His people, and desiring to come to their rescue, He resolved to descend upon earth in the form of a prophet, that He might lead them back into the path of safety.

The condition of things at this time justified the belief that the arrival of Jesus was signalized, imminent and necessary.

This explains why the Buddhist traditions affirm that the Eternal Spirit separated itself from the Eternal Being and incarnated itself into the newly-born child of a pious and noble family.

No doubt, the Buddhists as well as the Evangelists wished to indicate by this that the child belonged to the royal house of David, but the text of the Evangel, according to which the child was conceived of the Holy Ghost, can be interpreted in two ways, while according to the doctrine of Buddha, which is most conformable to the laws of nature, the Spirit only incarnated itself in a child already born, whom God blessed and chose to accomplish His mission here below.[4]

At this place there is a gap in the traditions of the Evangelists, who, either from ignorance or negligence, tell us nothing of his infancy, his youth or his training. They commence the history of Jesus with his first sermon, that is to say, at the time when at the age of thirty he returns to his country.

All that the Evangelists say concerning the childhood of Jesus totally lacks precision. "And the child grew and waxed strong, filled with wisdom, and the grace of God was upon him," says one of the sacred authors, St. Luke; and again: "The child grew and waxed strong in spirit, and was in the desert until the day of his showing unto Israel."

As the records of the Evangelists were compiled long after the death of Jesus, it is probable that they only consigned to writing the accounts of the principal events of his life.

On the contrary, the Buddhists, who recorded their chronicles soon after the crucifixion, and who had the advantage of collecting the most correct references to all points which interested them, give us a complete and detailed description of the life of Jesus.

In those unfortunate days, when the struggle for existence seems to have destroyed all notion of God, the people of Israel endured the double oppression of the ambitious Herod and the despotic and avaricious Romans. Then, as now, the Hebrews placed all their hope in Providence, who, they believed, would

---

[4]The theory of the Divinity or Buddha incarnating at different times is common to the Tibetan Buddhism and modern Hinduism. It is known as the Avatara theory. The head Lama of certain monasteries in Tibet is considered the living visible embodiment, for the time being, of Buddha, who from time to time descends from heaven and reappears in human forms for the welfare of the world. Krishna, in the Bhagvad Gita, says: "Every time that religion is in danger and that iniquity triumphs, I issue forth. For the defense of the good and the suppression of the wicked, for the establishment of righteousness, I manifest myself from age to age." And among the Buddhists there are various ranks in the incarnations; there are lower and higher Avataras, corresponding to the difference in rank of saints, etc.—Translator.

send them an inspired man, who would deliver them from their physical and moral sufferings. But time passed and no one took the initiative in a revolt against the tyranny of their rulers.

In these times of trouble and hope, the people of Israel forgot completely that there existed in their midst a poor Israelite who was directly descended from their King David. This poor man married a maiden who gave birth to a marvelous child.

The Hebrews heard of this, and faithful to their traditions of devotion and respect for the race of their kings, they went in crowds to congratulate the happy father and see the child. It is evident that Herod did not long remain ignorant of all that occurred. He feared that the child, when of age, would make use of his popularity to regain the throne of his ancestors. He therefore had search made for the child, whom the Israelites tried to conceal from the anger of the king; then he ordered the abominable massacre of the children, hoping that Jesus would perish in this vast human hecatomb, but the family of Joseph, being warned of the terrible execution that Herod contemplated, took refuge in Egypt.

Sometime afterwards they returned to their native land. The child had grown during these travels, although it had been exposed to many dangers. Then, as at present, the Oriental Israelites commenced the education of their children at the age of five or six years. Obliged always to remain concealed, the parents did not permit the son to leave the house; so, without doubt, he passed all his time studying the sacred writings, by which reason when he returned to Judea he was far in advance of all youths of his age, which greatly astonished the learned elders. He was in his thirteenth year, the age when, according to the Judaic law, a young man reaches majority and has the right to marry and perform his religious duties just as adults do.

There still exists among the Israelites an ancient religious custom which fixes the majority for males at thirteen, when the youth becomes a member of society and enjoys equal rights with the adults. Thus his marriage at this age is lawful, and is even indispensable in the warm countries. In Europe, however, this custom has fallen into desuetude and has no more importance, owing to the influence of local laws and also to the laws of nature, which do not contribute here so powerfully to the physical development of the young as in warmer countries.

His royal origin, his rare intelligence, and the hard study to which he had applied himself, caused even the most noble and wealthy people to regard him as an excellent match, and many strove to secure him for a son-in-law. Thus the Israelites of today hold it as an honor to marry their daughters to the son of a Rabbi or of a scholar. But the pensive youth, seemingly separated from all corporeal things, and with a great thirst for knowledge, left secretly the house of his parents and joined the caravans that were just leaving the country.

We may believe that Jesus Christ preferred to go to India, because at this time Egypt itself was a part of the Roman possessions, and also because a very brisk commercial exchange with India had circulated throughout Judea stories concerning the majestic character and the unheard-of richness of the arts and sciences in this marvellous country, whither even now all the aspirations of the civilized world turn.

Here the Evangelists lose the thread of the terrestrial life of Jesus. Luke says: "He remained in the desert until the time of showing unto Israel," which is a conclusive proof that no one knew where the young man had disappeared to, or whence he returned suddenly after sixteen years' absence.

On his arrival in India, the country of marvels, Jesus began to frequent the temples of the Jains. There has existed, and still exists, in the peninsula of Hindustan, a sect which bears the name of Jains; it forms, as it were, a bond of union between Buddhism and Brahmanism, and preaches the destruction of all other beliefs, which it declares are in error. It arose in the seventh century B.C. Its name is derived from the word "Jina," (conqueror) which is given as a symbol of triumph over its rivals.[5]

---

[5] In regard to the Jains of India, M. Notovitch seems to have followed the groundless assumption of some European scholars, that Jainism is a bond of union between Buddhism and Brahmanism; nay, some of the scholars maintained some years ago, that Jainism was a branch of Buddhism. But careful investigations have exploded that theory, and even the European scholars now hold that Jainism is older than Buddhism. In truth, accepting the

Astonished at the genius of the young man the Jainas requested him to remain in their midst; but Jesus left them to establish himself in Jagannath, where he devoted himself to the study of treatises of religion, philosophy, etc. Jagannath is one of the principal cities sacred to the Brahmins, and in the time of Christ possessed a great religious influence.[6]

At Jagannath there is a very fine library of precious Sanskrit books and religious manuscripts. Jesus remained six years here studying the language of the country and Sanskrit, which enabled him to search into all the religious doctrines, philosophy, medicine and mathematics. He found much to condemn in the Brahmanical customs and laws, and he maintained public discussions with the Brahmins who tried to convince him of the sacred character of their established customs.

Among other things Jesus denounced the injustice of humiliating the laborer (they not only deprived him of the right of future happiness, but also denied him the right to attend religious sermons). And Jesus began to preach to the Shudras, the lowest caste of slaves, teaching them that there is one God only according to their own laws, that all there is exists only through Him, that with Him all are equal, and that the Brahmins had obscured the great principle of monotheism in perverting the words of Brahma himself, and in insisting strongly on the external ceremonies.

According to the doctrines of the Brahmins, this is what God speaks of Himself to the angels: "I have been since eternity and forever will I be; I am the first cause of all that exists in the east and in the west, in the north and in the south, above and below,

---

general opinion that the Brahmins first came to India from the northwestern passes, the Jains are the descendants of the original owners of India, whom the Brahmins in their Vedas give all sorts of names, and who often disturbed them in their animal sacrifices. For further information on this subject, I refer the reader to my work on India.—Translator.

[6] Tradition claims that the ashes of the illustrious Brahmin Krishna are preserved here in the hollow of a tree near a magnificent temple. Krishna lived 1580 B.C., and collected and arranged the Vedas, which he divided into four books—Rik, Yajur, Saman and Atharvan. Krishna, who received for his work the name of Vyasa (i.e., he who has collected and divided the Vedas) has also composed the Vedenta and eighteen Puranas consisting of 400,000 stanzas.

Leh, as seen from outside the city (*See page 16.*)

in heaven and in hell. I am older than all things, I am the All-Powerful; I am the God of Gods; the King of Kings; I am Parabrahma, the great soul of the universe."

After the world had appeared by the mere desire of Parabrahma, God created men whom He arranged in four classes according to their color; white (Brahmins), red (Kshatriyas), yellow (Vaishyas) and black (Shudras).

Brahma drew the first from his own mouth and gave them as their portion the government of the world, the duty of teaching the men the laws and healing and of judging them. As the Brahmins only occupy the offices of priests, teachers and commentators of the Vedas, they alone should observe celibacy.

The second caste, that of the Kshatriyas, came from the hand of Brahma. He made them warriors, entrusting to them the care of defending society. All kings, princes, captains, governors and warlike people, belong to this caste, and preserve with the Brahmins the most cordial relations, because the one can not exist without the other, and because the peace of the country depends on the alliance of knowledge with power, of the temple of Brahma with the royal throne.

The Vaishyas, who form the third caste, were created by Brahma from his belly. They are destined to till the land, to raise cattle and carry on all kinds of trade and commerce, that they may support the Brahmins and the Kshatriyas. They are permitted to go to the temple and to listen to the readings of Vedas only on feast days; at other times they are obliged to attend to their allotted duties.

The last class, the blacks or Shudras, came from the feet of Brahma to be the humble servants or slaves of the other three castes. They are forbidden to attend the reading of the Vedas; he who comes in contact with them is defiled. They are miserable beings deprived of all human rights, not being allowed to look at members of the higher castes, and in sickness forbidden to receive a physician's care.

Death alone can free them from the consequences of their life of servitude; in order to get this reward, however, they must have served for their whole life, without murmur or idleness, a member of one of the privileged classes. Then, only, after having performed with fidelity and zeal his duties in the service of a Brahmin or a Kshatriya, has the Shudra the promise that his soul, after death, will be raised to a superior caste.

If a Shudra fails in his obedience towards a member of the privileged class or otherwise becomes disgraced, he is outcasted and degraded to the rank of a Paria, who is banished from all the towns and villages; he is the object of general scorn, is considered an abject creature, permitted to perform only the basest labor.

The same punishment may also be inflicted on a member of the other caste; but he, however, by repenting, fasting and penances can re-enter his former rank in the caste, while the unfortunate Shudra, once driven from his caste, is forever lost.

This explains the worship, by the Vaishyas and the Shudras, of Jesus, who although menaced by the Brahmins and Kshatriyas, continued teaching them.

Now, Jesus in his sermons censured not only the injustice of depriving a man of his rights as a man, and the worship of a monkey, a piece of marble or metal, but, also, he condemned the very principle of Brahmanism, its system of gods, its doctrines and its Trimurti, the corner stone of that religion.

Parabrahma is represented with three faces upon one head; this is the Trimurti composed of Brahma, the creator, Vishnu, the preserver and Shiva, the destroyer.

The origin of the Trimurti is:

In the beginning Parabrahma created the waters and in them cast the generative seed which transformed itself into a glowing egg reflecting the image of Brahma. Millions of centuries passed by when Brahma divided the egg into two parts, one of which, the upper half, became the sky, the lower half, the earth. This done, Brahma descended on earth in the form of a child seating himself on a lotus-flower, and there began to ponder within himself thus: Who will watch over and preserve what I have created? An answer came from his mouth in the form of a flame "I." And Brahma gave to this word the name Vishnu, which means "he who preserves." Then Brahma divided his being into two parts, the one male, the other female—the active world and the passive world—the union of which gave birth to Shiva, the destroyer.

The following are the attributes of the Trimurti: Brahma, the creative being; Vishnu, the preserving wisdom; Shiva, the destructive wrath of Justice. Brahma is the substance of which everything is made, Vishnu the space in which all things live, and Shiva the time which annihilates all things. Brahma, the air which invigorates all, Vishnu, the water which sustains the strength of creatures; Shiva, the fire which breaks the bond that unites all things. Brahma is the past, Vishnu the present, and Shiva the future. Each part of the Trimurti possesses also a wife. That of Brahma is Sarasvati, goddess of wisdom; that of Vishnu is Lakshmi, goddess of virtue; and Shiva is wedded to Kali, the goddess of death, the universal destroyer.

From this last union was born the wise god Ganesha, and Indra, chief of the inferior divinities; the number of which including all objects of worship of the Hindus reaches three hundred millions.

Vishnu came down upon earth eight times, incarnating himself first in a fish, to save the sacred books from the deluge, then successively in a tortoise, a dwarf, a wild boar, a lion, then in Rama, who was a king's son, in Krishna and finally in Buddha. He will come for the ninth time in the form of a cavalier mounted upon a white horse to destroy death and sin.

Jesus denied the existence of all these hierarchical absurdities of God, which obscured the great principle of monotheism.

The Brahmins, seeing that the people began to adopt the doctrines of Jesus, their opponent whom they had hoped to win to themselves, resolved to kill him; but being warned by his faithful followers of the dangers menacing him, he fled to the mountains of Nepal.

Buddhism had taken deep roots in this country at this period. This schism was remarkable on account of its moral principles and ideas on the nature of divinity—ideas which brought man and nature, and men among themselves nearer together.

The founder of this sect, Shakya Muni, was born 1500 B.C., at Kapila, the capital of his father's kingdom, near Nepal in the Himalayas. He belonged to the race of the Gautamides and to the ancient family of the Shakyas. From his infancy he displayed a great interest in religion, and, contrary to the wishes of his father, he left the palace with all its alluring luxuries and began to preach against the Brahmins, purifying their doctrines. He died at Kushinagara surrounded by many faithful disciples. His body was burned and his ashes were distributed among the villages from which his new doctrine had driven Brahmanism.

According to the Buddhist doctrine, the Creator always remains in a condition of perfect inaction which nothing can disturb and from which He emerges, only at times determined by fate in order to create earthly Buddhas. To this end the Spirit separates itself from the sovereign Creator, and becomes incarnated in a Buddha and dwells upon the earth for some time, where it creates Bodhisattvas (masters), whose mission it is to preach the divine law and to found new churches of believers, to whom they give laws and for whom they institute a new religious order, following the traditions of Buddhism.

An earthly Buddha is, in several ways, a reflection of the sovereign Creator Buddha, to whom he is united again after having ended his life upon earth; the Bodhisattvas, too, as a reward for their labor and for the privations which they have endured here below, receive eternal happiness and enjoy a repose which nothing can disturb.[7]

Jesus sojourned six years among the Buddhists, where he found the principle of monotheism still in its purity. Having attained the age of twenty-six years, he remembered his native land which was under the heavy oppression of foreigners. He therefore resolved to return there. On his journey he preached in many countries against idolatry, human sacrifices and religious errors, exhorting the people to recognize and worship God, the Father of all beings whom He loved equally, the masters as well as the slaves, for they are all His children, to whom He has given His beautiful universe as a common heritage. The sermons of Jesus often produced a deep impression upon the people through whose country he journeyed, exposed to all sorts of dangers instigated against him by the clergy, but protected by

---

[7] This, in purport is true, about the Tibetan Buddhism, which differs in many respects from the Southern Buddhism.—Translator.

the idolators who had only the day before offered their children as sacrifices to their idols.

While crossing Persia, Jesus almost caused a revolt among the worshipers of the doctrine of Zoroaster. The priests, fearing the vengeance of the people, dared not assassinate him; they resorted to stratagem and drove him from the city at night, hoping that the fierce beasts would devour him, but Jesus escaped this peril and arrived safe and sound in the country of Israel.

It is to be remarked here that the Orientals sometimes so picturesque in the midst of their miseries and the ocean of corruption in which they have sunk under the constant influences of their priests and teachers, possess, nevertheless, a pronounced taste for instruction and easily understand proper explanations. More than once, by using simple words of truth I appealed to the conscience of a robber or a rebellious servant. These people, filled with the sentiment of innate honesty which the priests, to further their personal ends, make every endeavor to crush, very quickly become honest and feel contempt for those who have unjustly abused them.

By the single virtue of truthfulness one could make of entire India with its three hundred millions of idols a vast Christian country. But this beautiful project would probably create a prejudice among certain Christians, who like the priests above mentioned, speculate upon the ignorance of the masses to enrich themselves.

St. Luke says that Jesus was about thirty years old when he entered on his ministry. According to the Buddhist chronicler Jesus must have begun preaching in his twenty-ninth year. All his sermons which the evangelists do not mention and which have been preserved by the Buddhists are remarkable for their character of divine grandeur. The fame of the new preacher spread rapidly through the country and Jerusalem eagerly awaited his arrival. When he approached the holy city, the people went to meet him in great throngs and led him triumphantly to the temple, which is in conformity with the Christian tradition. The chiefs and the learned men who heard him, admired his sermons and rejoiced at the beneficent impression

Leh, as seen from the market-place (*See page 16.*)

produced by his words on the multitude. All the remarkable sermons of Jesus are full of sublime words.

Pilate, the governor of the country, however, did not look at this matter in the same light. Zealous agents reported to him that Jesus had announced the near approach of a new kingdom, the re-establishment of the throne of Israel, and that he claimed himself to be the Son of God, sent to restore the courage of Israel, for he, the King of Judea, would soon ascend the throne of his ancestors.

I do not wish to attribute to Jesus the role of revolutionist, but it seems to me very probable that Jesus worked upon the people with the view of re-establishing the throne which belonged to him by right of inheritance. Divinely inspired and at the same time convinced that his pretentions were legitimate, Jesus preached the spiritual union of the people in order that a political union might result.

Alarmed at these rumors, Pilate called the learned men and the elders of the people together and ordered them to forbid Jesus to preach publicly, and even to condemn him in the temple under the charge of apostasy. This was the best way of ridding himself of a dangerous man, of whose royal origin Pilate knew and whose fame was increasing among the people.

We must remark here that far from persecuting Jesus the Israelites recognizing in him the descendant of the illustrious dynasty of David, made him the object of their secret hopes, as is proven by the Scriptures which relate that Jesus preached freely and openly in the temple in the presence of the elders, who could have forbidden him not only access to the temple, but even more, the right to preach.

By Pilate's order, the Sanhedrim met and summoned Jesus to appear before its tribunal. At the close of the inquest the members of the Sanhedrim informed Pilate that his suspicions were groundless, as Jesus made only a religious propaganda and not a political one; that he preached the divine word and that furthermore he claimed to have come not to overthrow, but to re-establish the laws of Moses. The Buddhist chronicle only confirms the sympathy which undoubtedly existed between

Jesus, the young preacher, and the elders of Israel. Hence their reply, "we will not judge a just man."

Pilate was not satisfied, however, and sought another opportunity to bring Jesus before a new and regular tribunal; with this object a number of spies were sent to watch him and finally apprehended him.

According to the Evangelists, it was the Pharisees and the Hebrews who sought to put Jesus to death, while the Buddhist chronicle declares positively that Pilate alone was responsible. This latter version is evidently much more probable than the former; the conquerors of Judea could not long tolerate the presence of a man who announced to the people their near deliverance from the foreign yoke. Undoubtedly, the popularity of Jesus was alarming to Pilate, who, to insure his own safety, naturally surrounded the young preacher with his crafty agents instructed to watch his every word and action. They tried by putting embarrassing questions to Jesus to draw from him imprudent words which would serve as an excuse for Pilate's anger. If the teaching of Jesus had displeased the learned men and Hebrew priests, they would simply have forbidden the people to listen to him or follow him and would have prevented him from entering the temple. The Evangelists, however, relate that Jesus enjoyed great liberty among the Israelites, and in the temples where Pharisees and wise men conversed with him.

In order to insure the condemnation of Jesus, Pilate submitted him to preliminary tortures to force from him an avowal of high treason. These tortures did not produce the desired result. But, contrary to the usual experience with other innocent prisoners subjected to like sufferings, Jesus remained firm, never faltering or speaking the slightest words by which he could be condemned. Thus finding himself foiled, Pilate commanded that Jesus be put to the utmost tortures, hoping to hasten death by exhausting his vital forces. Jesus, however, using his great will to increase his strength and courage, and having confidence in his just cause which was that of the nation and of God, endured with great fortitude all the bitter cruelties of his executioners. The secret and extraordinary tortures provoked discontent among the elders, who therefore resolved to intercede in his favor and demand that he be set free before the feast of Passover. Their demand being rejected by Pilate, they insisted that he be brought before the tribunal, so certain were they of his acquittal which seemed the more sure since the entire people ardently desired it.

In the eyes of the priests, Jesus was a saint belonging to the family of David, and his unjust imprisonment or that which was much more serious, his condemnation, would cast a profound gloom over the solemnities of the great national festival of the Israelites. Learning of the refusal of their demands, they begged that the judgment might take place before the festival. To this Pilate acceded, but he also caused two robbers to be judged at the same time. By this method Pilate endeavored to weaken in the eyes of the people the importance of the fact that the tribunal had tried and rendered judgment against an innocent man alone, which would leave on the minds of the entire nation the sad impression that a verdict had been planned in advance. On the contrary, the condemnation of Jesus simultaneously with that of the thieves would almost efface the injustice committed against one of the prisoners.

The accusation was founded upon the evidence of hired witnesses.

During the trial, Pilate perverted the words of Jesus (which taught of the kingdom of Heaven) to justify the accusation which was formulated against him. He reckoned, it would seem, on the effect produced by the answers of Jesus and upon his personal authority to influence the members of the tribunal not to examine too minutely the details of the case in hand to secure a verdict according to his desire.

After having heard the perfectly natural answer of the judges that the words of Jesus were diametrically opposed to the accusation, and therefore he could not be condemned thereon, Pilate had no other recourse but to employ, the evidence of an informer who, as the Governor thought, could not fail to produce a very strong impression upon the judges. This wretch, who was none other than Judas, formally accused Jesus of having aroused a revolt among the people.

Then took place a scene most sublime. When Judas gave his evidence, Jesus turned to him, and having blessed him, said: "Thou shalt be forgiven, for what thou sayest cometh not of thee"; then addressing the Governor, he said: "Why humiliate thy dignity and teach thy inferiors to live in falsehood, since even without this thou hast the power to condemn an innocent person?"—Words sublime and touching! Jesus Christ manifests himself there in all his grandeur by convincing first the informer of having sold his conscience, then by pardoning him. Afterwards he addresses Pilate, reproaching him for having had recourse to a process so degrading to his dignity to obtain his condemnation. The accusation that Jesus made against Pilate caused the Governor to completely forget his position and prudence which he should have displayed. So he demanded imperiously of the judges the condemnation of Jesus, and as if to assert his unlimited power, he ordered the acquittal of the robbers. The judges, finding this demand of Pilate that would force them to acquit the robbers and condemn Jesus though innocent, too unjust for them to comply with, refused to commit this double crime against their conscience and their laws. But being unable to contend against him who had the power to pronounce a final and unappealable verdict, and seeing that he was determined on ridding himself, at any cost, of a man for whom the Roman authorities had the slightest suspicion, they left him to pronounce the verdict which he had so much at heart. That they might not suffer the reproaches of the people, who would never have forgiven them for such great injustice, they washed their hands in the presence of the people as they left the tribunal hall, thus showing that they had not sanctioned the death of the just Jesus whom the people worshiped.

About ten years ago I read in a German journal, the "Fremdenblatt," an article on Judas, in which the author showed that the informer had been the best friend of Jesus. It was for love of his master that Judas had betrayed him, believing blindly in the words of the Saviour, who said that his kingdom would come after his death. But when he beheld him on the cross, Judas, after having vainly awaited the promised resurrection, could not overcome his overwhelming remorse, and hung himself. It is useless to elaborate on this lucubration, though it is certainly original enough.

But to return to the scriptural narrative and to the Buddhist chronicle, it is quite probable that the hired informer was Judas, although upon this point the Buddhist version is silent. As to the theory that remorse of conscience led the informer to take his own life, I do not attach any credit to it. A man capable of committing such a cowardly act and of accusing a friend falsely and that without any spirit of envy or revenge, but only for a handful of silver, such a man, I say, is psychologically valueless and incapable of knowing what honesty or conscience is, therefore remorse is unknown to him. It is probable that the Governor acted in this matter, as is done sometimes in our own day when it is necessary to conceal from the people a grave secret at any cost, and had Judas hanged immediately, to prevent the truth from ever being revealed to the public that the testimony which condemned Jesus emanated from Pilate alone.

On the day of the execution, a large detachment of Roman soldiers was stationed around the cross to prevent the crowd from rescuing the object of their worship. In this Pilate displayed extraordinary firmness and resolution. Owing to these precautions, sedition was arrested; he could not, however, hinder the people weeping over the death of their cherished idol, he being the last branch of the descendant of David.

Great throngs went to worship the tomb of Jesus. Although we have no definite account concerning the first days following the execution, we can, by probable conjectures, reconstruct the scenes which must have followed. It is very probable that the prudent lieutenant of the Roman Cæsar, seeing that the tomb of Jesus had become a place of universal lamentation and national grief, and fearing that the memory of the just man would excite the discontent and raise the entire country against the foreign yoke, should employ all possible means to banish the remembrance of Jesus from the mind of the public. Pilate caused the body of Jesus to be buried near the place of execution and placed a detachment of soldiers on guard, who for three days were the jest and scorn of the people, who, braving the danger, came in throngs to worship the great martyr. Then

Pilate ordered the soldiers to raise the body by night, when the pilgrimage ceased, and to bury it secretly in some other place, leaving the first tomb open and unguarded so that the people might see that Jesus had disappeared. But Pilate failed to accomplish this purpose; for the next day, not finding the body of their Master in the sepulcher, the Hebrews who were superstitious and believed in miracles, declared that he had arisen from the dead. How this legend ever came to be so generally accepted, we do not know; perhaps it remained latent for a long time and then spread among low people. Possibly the Ecclesiastical authorities among the Hebrews looked upon this innocent belief with indulgence, which gave the oppressed a shadow of revenge against their oppressors. Howsoever this may be, since the day when this legend of the resurrection of Jesus became known to all, no one has been firm enough to point out the impossibility of it.

Concerning the resurrection we must notice that according to the Buddhists the soul of the just unites itself to the Eternal Being, while the Evangelists insist rather upon the ascension of the body. It seems to me, nevertheless, that the Evangelists and the Apostles were very wise in giving a plastic description of the resurrection, for otherwise, i.e., if the miracle had been less material, their teachings would not have had, in the eyes of the people, that divine authority, that character so manifestly divine, which Christianity retains even today, as being the only religion capable of maintaining the people in a condition of sublime enthusiasm, of softening their savage instincts, and of bringing them nearer the grand and simple nature which God has entrusted, it is said, to that feeble dwarf called "man."